Oleg Pomoshnikov, Jan Radziemski

The Russian Destroyer Spravedlivyy 1956

KAGERO

Starboard side view.

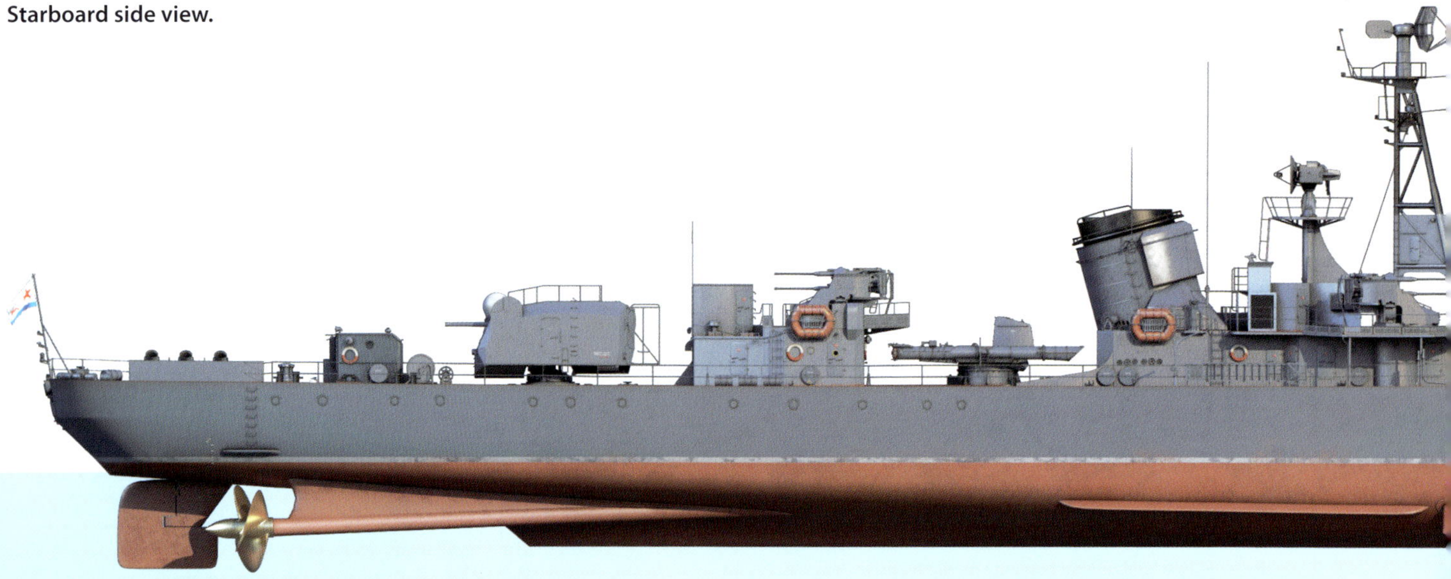

Introduction

The first Polish missile destroyer to bear the name ORP *Warszawa* was built in Leningrad and initially served under the name *Spravedlivyy*. In her original form she was an old-fashioned destroyer armed with guns and torpedoes and was only converted into a missile destroyer after more than a decade of intense service. Shortly afterward, she was sold to the Polish Navy and had her hull adorned with the name of the Polish capital.

The history of the ship in the Soviet Navy

The destroyer *Spravedlivyy* was constructed in the Severniy Sudostroitelniy Zavod imeni A.A. Zhdanova (Shipyard No. 190) in 1954–1956 as one of 27 Project 56 destroyers, also known as the *Spokoinyy* class (designated *Kotlin* by NATO). They were destroyers in the old fashion, created in the early 1950s by designers of the 53rd Central Design Bureau (CKB-53) led by head designer A.L. Fisher, who was also the author of Project 30bis (NATO: *Skoryy*-class).

Project 56 destroyers were vessels of supreme pulchritude and grace, with a smooth deck and highly elevated, forward-leaning prow evoking a sense of speed. The upper deck provided room for three large superstructures, two light cage masts and a pair of wide, slightly slanted funnels. The forward superstructure was crowned with the distinctive SBP-42-56 command and rangefinder station with the Yakor-M radar. A Fut-B fire-control radar was located in front of it with another such radar positioned on a platform between the mainmast and the aft funnel. At the moment of commissioning the displacement of the destroyer was 2,667 tonnes standard and 3,230 full. The length of the hull was 126.1 meters. The armament consisted of four 130 mm naval guns split between two light turrets, one on the bow and one on the stern. The anti-aircraft armament comprised four quadruple mounts of 45 mm guns. The ship was also equipped with two torpedo launchers for 533 mm torpedoes (five tubes per launcher) as well as mine-laying racks. For anti-submarine warfare the ship was provided with six depth charge throwers and depth charge racks on the stern.

As was typical for Soviet destroyers, the ship was propelled by steam turbines which provided 72,000 horsepower and let the vessel reach a speed of 38.5 knots. A meticulously designed hull improved the seakeeping ability of the ship. The design—higher sides and upper deck wider at the bow than was the case in her predecessors—was retained for many years in subsequent ship classes: Projects 58, 1134, and 1134A. It is worth noting that one of the Soviet admirals argued in favor of copying the hull design of *Novik*-class destroyers, which had originated before World War One! Obviously, the hull design, flawless though it might be, will not provide speed in and of itself, so an "upgrade" of the propulsion was envisaged. Improvements in the turbine design and efficiency of the boilers increased the power, which was then transferred to two three-bladed propellers.

Service In the Soviet Navy

After being commissioned the ship was transferred to the Baltic Fleet and became part of the 128th Destroyer Brigade. From 1961 until 1964 she was used for combat training and in the mid-1960s she was periodically assigned to operational deployments. Throughout October 1964 she monitored exercises in the North Sea and Norwegian Sea (FOLEX 64) and she spent the period from April until June 1968 in the Norwegian Sea and North Atlantic. While serving in the Soviet Navy she made port visits in Copenhagen, Denmark, (8–12 May 1964) and Rostock, German Democratic Republic, (18–22 October 1962). Throughout her service she bore many hull numbers: 92 (1956), 254 (1959), 256 (1960), 254 (1963?), 191 (1964), 954 (1965), 175 (1967), 375 (1969), and 372 (1970).

Conversion to Project 56A

In the summer of 1956 CKB-7 began working on the M-1 anti-aircraft system (later known as Volna), designed specifically for surface vessels. The system was tested on the Project 56K destroyer *Bravyy* to satisfying results and was accepted into service in 1962. However, since the vessels that were supposed to carry the system were not yet ready, a decision was made to re-arm some of the Project 56 destroyers. The decision was made easier in light of developments on the other side of the Atlantic. The Americans had commenced testing the Terrier guided surface-to-air missile system as early as 1956, utilizing the *Gearing*-class destroyer USS *Gyatt* (DD 712/DDG-1). Moreover, the US Navy commissioned a series of 23 *Charles F. Adams*-class destroyers in the early 1960s, each equipped with a single launcher for the Tartar SAM system. The best way of countering the American advantage was through a rapid modification of *Spokoinyy*-class destroyers and arming them with SAMs of their own. N.P. Sobolev's CKB-53 designed such a modification, which would improve the destroyers' capabilities both in the AA and ASW fields. On 25 October 1964 the project was approved, designated 56A.

Work on the first ship commenced the following year. The destroyer *Spravedlivyy* was modernized to Project 56A standards in the Severniy Sudostroitelniy Zavod imeni A.A. Zhdanova (Shipyard No. 190); work began on 14 May 1966 and ended on 2 November 1969. The vessel lost a significant part of her armament: the first torpedo launcher and everything astern of it was removed (i.e. the other PTA-53-56 launcher,

three 45 mm SM-20-ZIF autocannon mounts and the aft SM-2-1 turret), as was the mainmast with all the antennae. The mine racks were also removed. The aft superstructure was redesigned with a reinforced deck and a plate to serve as a blast deflector for missiles being launched. These changes provided significant savings on mass and removed the need for redesigning the aft funnel.

The removed armament was replaced with a double launcher of Volna SAMs with two cylindrical magazines, each housing eight missiles. A new mast, this time a full pyramid mast, provided a base for the antennae of the Yatagan fire control system, which guided the missiles. A new MR-310 Angara search radar was installed on the foremast. The ASW armament of the destroyer was also improved through the installation of two RBU-6000 launchers (RBU-2500 on the *Spravedlivyy* and *Skromnyy*) with the Burya-56A fire control system, but the obsolete Pegas-2M sonar was retained. The outline of the stern was changed to be more rounded and depth charge racks were removed from under the deck, as was the 1-tonne stern anchor.

The modifications brought about an increase in displacement by circa 380–400 tonnes and, in turn, a drop in speed. The stability of the vessel was worsened due to the mass of new, elevated components, which then had to be compensated with additional ballast. However, since there was no room to add it, fuel had to be used for this purpose, and this meant that range would decrease. Project 56A destroyers were also provided with a completely new solution: each boiler compartment was fitted with airtight cabins from which the main mechanisms could be operated remotely.

The modified Project 56 destroyers (designated *Kotlin-SAM* by NATO) became the Soviet Navy's first ships armed with guided anti-aircraft missiles. As a result, Project 56A destroyers became more versatile, but while they gained a new potential in fighting airborne targets, ASW equipment remained their Achilles heel due to the ancient sonar. The modification also brought about a significant change in the overall outline of the destroyers.

Purchase by the Polish Navy

The Polish Navy had been considering equipping its ships with missiles since 1956. There was, however, no way that the Poles could do it on their own. They needed the "Big Brother" to agree, and he was not keen on providing them with modern weapon systems. Therefore, talks which began in mid-1960s were initially futile. When the Polish Navy brass mentioned their desire to purchase a destroyer of a new class, the commander of the Soviet Navy, Admiral Sergey Georgiyevich Gorshkov, quickly cut them down to size, stating that Poles have no need for destroyers armed with anti-ship missiles. During protracted negotiations the Soviets changed their mind over an over again. At one point they refused to sell a Project 56 destroyer, then they showed willingness to sell a Project 61 destroyer and quickly backtracked.

The negotiations picked up pace after 1967, when destroyers in Polish service at the time were approaching the end of their useful life and one of them, ORP *Błyskawica*, suffered a malfunction. Thus, when the Russians offered to provide the Polish Navy with a Project 56A destroyer, even though they had newer and more potent ships at their disposal, the Poles had to accept. The decision to proceed with the purchase was made in 1969 and soon a group of Polish sailors was sent to Leningrad for training. The eventual price of the ship was 952.3 million złotys, a large sum when one considers her age. The price included 48 V-601 missiles (plus three training missiles), five SET-53 torpedoes and 384 RGB-25 anti-submarine rockets. On transfer to the Polish Navy, the ship carried 14 live missiles and one training missile; the remainder were delivered by train.

Before the destroyer was transferred, she returned to her shipyard in 1970 to have some of her electronics gear replaced with less modern devices. Essentially, the 56AE ("E" for *eksportnyy*, or export) variant differed from the base Project 56A only in the electronics department. It was equipped with a 2D air search radar, the MR-300E Angara, instead of the more modern MR-310A Angara-A, which was a 3D radar. Additionally, the SM-2-1 gun turret was stripped of the Shtag-B radar rangefinder.

Design

The modernized Project 56A destroyers lost nothing of their pulchritude and retained their air of elegance and swiftness. Some would even say that the alterations made them look more aggressive. Still, Project 56A destroyers looked as if they had been created by gluing two different vessels into one: the fore part with its armament was straight out of the 1950s, but the rear half had a late-1960s look to it.

The welded hull was made of SKhL-1 low-carbon steel with type 3 steel used for less important partitions, foundations, and platforms. The hull skin had longitudinal supports and was thicker on the waterline along its entire length to enable movement through ice. The superstructures was made of duralumin to save on weight, but during sea trials warping and strong vibrations occurred, so it was necessary to reinforce the superstructures. The hull was divided into 16 watertight compartments. During storms it was possible to walk from stern to bow without going out onto the upper deck. The ship had two decks, upper and lower, with three platforms between them. The destroyer was able to remain afloat with any three adjacent compartments flooded (with the exception of the engine-boiler compartments where it was possible with two compartments flooded).

Port side view.

As was the case with previous projects—30bis and 41—the *Kotlins* were partially armored. The thickest armor (20–40 mm) was applied to the turrets. The combat control center, bridge, and torpedo launcher walls were protected by armor up to 10 mm in thickness. Ammunition magazines for the primary guns had no armor and were only protected from above by the reinforced deck under the SM-2-1 turrets and from the sides by the thicker ice-protection belt. Seakeeping ability was intended as one of their strongest suits. The prow was raised and so was the freeboard: to 12.2 m on the bow, 7.4 m amidships, and 7.65 m on the stern. The well designed shape of the hull, complemented with stabilizers, bilge keels, and two deep fuel tanks ensured stability and safe movement in any weather.

Propulsion

The engine rooms were arranged in an echelon in two autonomous compartments. Each compartment housed a set of TV-8 turbines, which provided 36,000 shaft horsepower, and two main KV-76 boilers, which produced steam at 450° C and 64 kgf/cm^2. In order to ensure the survivability of the engine rooms, their compartments were separated by two other compartments and one fuel tank. One TV-8 turbine set comprised two turbines: an active high-pressure turbine and a low-pressure backing turbine with a condenser and a double reduction gear with the main thrust bearing.

The automatized KV-41 boilers were vertical natural circulation water-tube boilers with air blast directed into the furnace. Airflow was provided by TVK-9 air blast units. The small size of the boiler—below 6 meters—made it possible to place two boilers in one compartment with a turbine set, with one boiler facing the other. The engine room could be operated quickly without pre-heating. The normal fuel supply was 280 tonnes of mazut, full supply: 560 tonnes. The ship was able to reach a speed of 34 knots (14 knots in astern propulsion, but full speed astern was as much as 19 knots). The range was 2,150 nautical miles at 17 knots and 588 nautical miles at 34 knots. The electric systems of the ship were powered by two TD-12 turbo-generators (400 kW each) and two DG-200/1 diesel generators (200 kW each), for a total power of 1,200 kW with a three-phase system of alternating current at 220 V and 50 Hz. The energy sources were divided between two powerplants, so as to increase survivability and reliability.

Armament

The Volna SAM system

The main weapon system of Project 56A destroyers was the M-1 Volna, which served as a means of eliminating airborne threats (both aircraft and missiles) in the close layer of air defense. The Volna was a derivative of the land-based S-125 Neva (NATO reporting name SA-3 Goa), which was operated by Poland within her Country Air Defense Forces.

The entire system comprised a ZIF-101 stabilized launcher with two rails from which missiles were launched; a missile magazine; a missile elevator; and the 4R90 Yatagan fire control system. The launcher could be traversed in the +/–330° range, elevated to +95° and depressed to –10° and with stabilization in the –20/+20° range. The launcher was traversed at 40°/second, elevated at 30°/second, and stabilized at 15°/second. The system was operated by 22 men. The V-601 (4K91) missiles were stored in two revolving magazines, eight in each. The missile, which entered service in 1968, was the successor of the earlier V-600, which had too small a range and was not capable enough when it came to destroying targets at small altitudes. The new missile utilized both a new engine and a new warhead: the 5B18, which had a mass of 78 kg and fragmented into circa 4,500 shards, significantly increasing the probability of destroying the target. The mass of the entire missile was 980 kg and its top speed was Mach 3 The V-601 increased the range of the system to 22 km and the flight altitude of its targets to 14 km (targets could be engaged at a distance of 100–14,000 m).

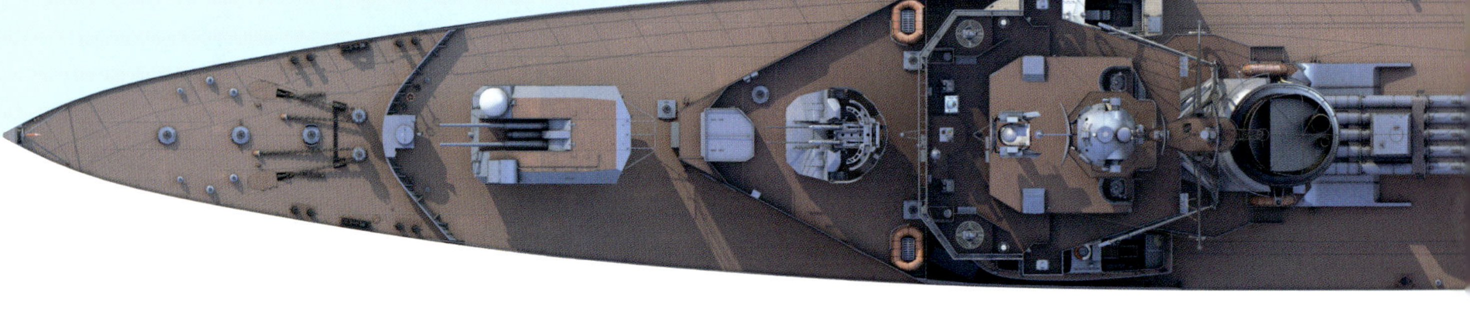

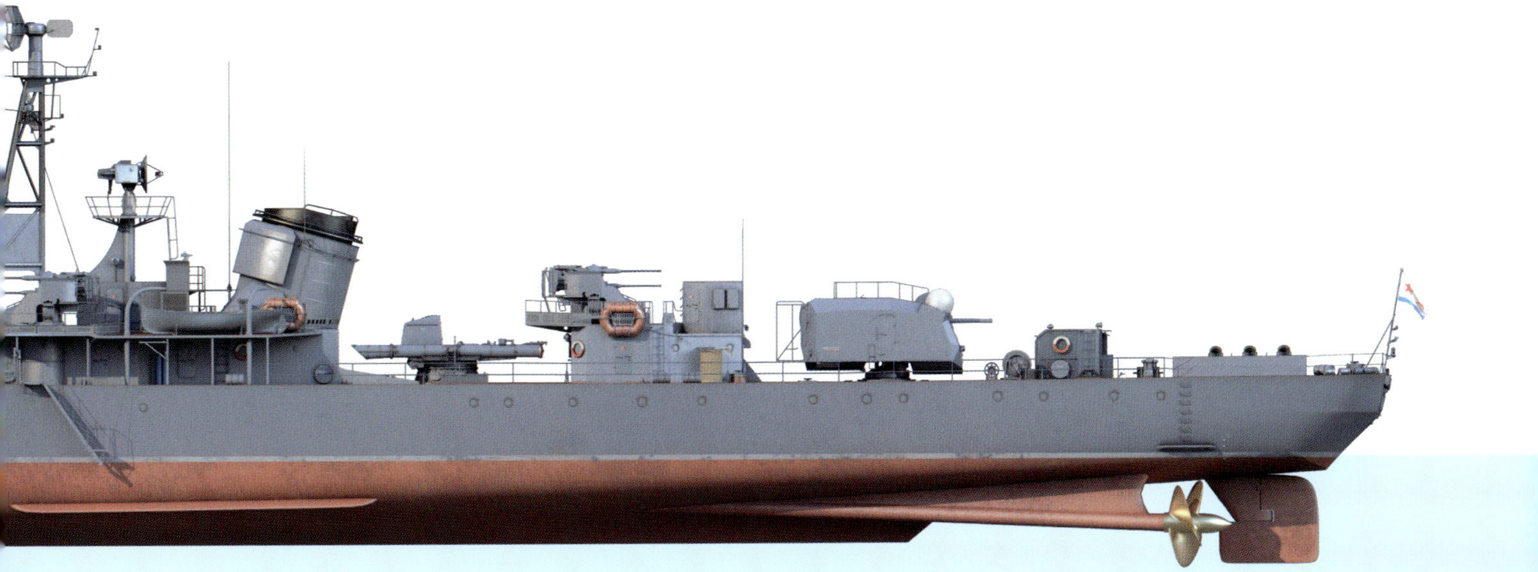

The Yatagan fire control system was also upgraded in 1967–1968. Moreover, the M-1 system was also adapted to attacking seaborne targets at small range; it was suited for this purpose due to its short reaction time. The missiles were guided by the five antennae of the Yatagan system. Two small antennae guided the missile in the initial flight stage, two large ones tracked the target and guided the missile towards it, and the final antenna relayed radio commands. As there was only one radio link for guidance, if both missiles were launched, they had to be directed at the same target. The system could operate in two modes: automatic and semi-automatic. The former was utilized, if the enemy was using jamming equipment. During trials the likelihood of intercepting a target—a MiG-17 fighter—at a distance of 42 km was calculated to be just 50% and at a distance of 36 km: 80%. Active jamming decreased these distances to 32 and 20 km, respectively. The M-1 system was able to engage targets moving at speed up to 700 meters per second (1,566 miles per hour).

Transitioning into the combat-ready position took five minutes and the first missile could be launched after six minutes from the moment the process started. After the first salvo the next round of missiles could be launched after 50 seconds (if the first pair was launched at the maximum distance of 22 km).

General characteristics upon transfer to the Polish Navy

Displacement (tonnes)	
standard	3,060
normal	3,340
full load	3,620
Length (meters)	126,2
Beam (meters)	12,8
Draught (meters)	4,4
Propulsion	4 KV-76 boilers, 2 TV-8 steam turbine sets, 72,000 hp, 2 propellers, 1 balanced rudder
Speed (knots)	
full ahead	34.5 (32.5)
economic	17
Range (naut. miles at knots)	2,150/17, 588/34
Endurance (days)	10
Armament	
missiles	1 × 2 ZIF-101 launchers for V-601 SAMs (16 missiles stored)
guns	1 × 2 130 mm SM-2-1 (525 rounds) 1 × 4 45 mm SM-20 (3,000 rounds)
torpedoes	1 × 5 MPTA-53-56M 533 mm torpedo launcher (5 torpedoes stored)
ASW	2 × 16 RBU-2500 rocket launcher for RGB-25 rocket depth charges (128 rocket depth charges stored)
Electronics	Don marine radar with Palma adapter, MR-300E Angara search radar, Yatagan SAM fire control radar, Yakor-2M fire control radar for the 130 mm guns, Fut-B fire control radar for the 45 mm guns, Pegas-2M sonar
Complement	266/268 (incl. 20 officers)

Artillery

The primary guns used on the destroyers were the double 130 mm/58 caliber SM-2-1 stabilized semi-automatic dual-purpose naval guns housed in two turrets, with two barrels per turret. The stabilization system was able to maintain the alignment of the guns at lists up to 15°. The turrets were protected by light armor: 20 mm at the front, 10 mm at the sides and roof. The turret roof was removable, but this, unfortunately, resulted in problems for the gun crews, especially in low temperatures or, in the case of the fore turret, during storms. The turret had a mass of 58.6 tonnes and was crewed by 21 men. The SM-2-1 guns were loaded manually and semi-automatically with separate-loading ammunition. The propellant charge was 1024.5 mm long and could reach a mass of 28 kg. The mass of the full powder charge was 15.3 kg. The mass of the shot was 60.5 kg. The projectile could be fired at a distance of 27.8 km and altitude of 21 km. Different sources provide different data on the rate of fire. Most likely, in the semi-automatic mode the rate of fire was 14 shots per minute against seaborne targets and 10 shots per minute against airborne targets. A single barrel was able to fire 54 projectiles

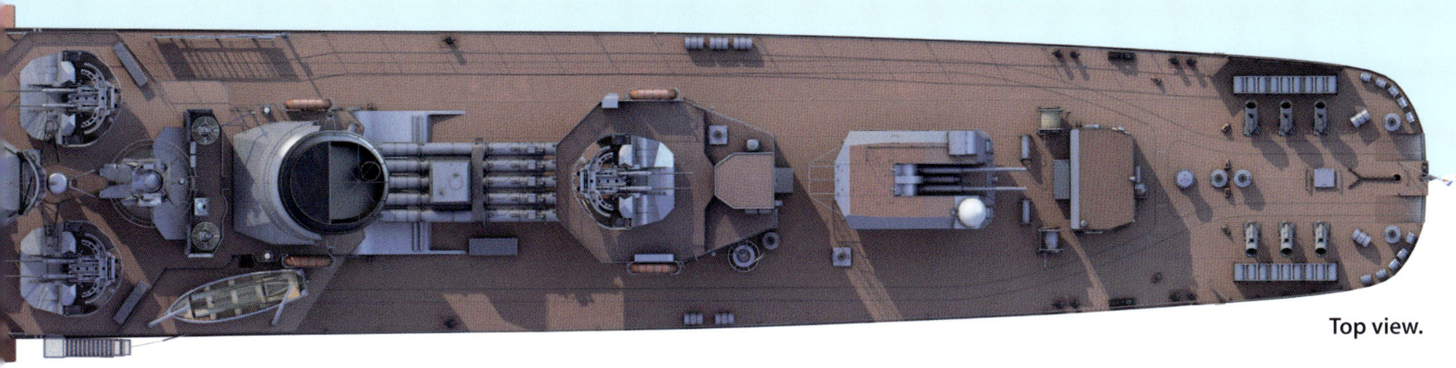

Top view.

without any pauses, after which it had to be cooled for 4–5 minutes. The ship could carry 400 shells in her magazine (the number could be increased to 525, if needed) plus 25 in cases for initial salvoes.

There was a wide range of ammunition at the ship's disposal: semi-armor-piercing, high-explosive dual-purpose, anti-aircraft with proximity fuze, anti-aircraft with spacer tube, illuminating with parachute, anti-radar, and training rounds. In the 1960s the guns were also provided with large-depth ASW rounds. The shot could be made with three charges: combat, combat reduced, and special, intended for illuminating rounds. The guns could be trained remotely (from the central artillery control station with the use of the remote D-2 system), semi-automatically, or manually. The firing solutions were provided by the Yakor-M radar supported by the stabilized SPV-42-50 guiding station with a DMS-3 rangefinder. The data gathered by all these devices were transferred to the Sfera-56 system, which performed the final calculations. The system enabled firing at airborne, seaborne, and coastal targets. The Yakor-M radar was able to detect aircraft at 35 km (in the subsequent model this distance grew to 44 km).

The anti-aircraft artillery comprised one SM-20 ZIF mount with quadruple 76 mm/45 caliber guns with the D-20 remote control system and backup VKM-45-4M reflector sights. The magazines contained 3,000 rounds with and additional 300 rounds in cases for initial salvoes. The ammunition supply consisted of both frag-tracer rounds and high explosive rounds. The rate of fire was 640 shots per minute for the entire mount (160 shots per minute per barrel). After 65 shots a barrel needed one minute to cool down. The ballistic range of the SM-20 ZIF was 11,000 m and the maximum altitude of fire was 7,900 m. The rounds were fitted with a self-destruct mechanism set for a distance of 6,700 m. The mass of the SM-20 ZIF was 14,9 tonnes and it was manned by 7 sailors, not counting those delivering ammunition. The guns were able to fire autonomously with the use of their own sights at a distance of up to 4,000 m. The fire control system comprised the Fut-N search radar (on the mainmast) for detecting airborne and seaborne targets as well as two Fut-B anti-aircraft fire control radars on the bridge and behind the mainmast. The radar were able to detect objects at ranges of up to 11 km and altitude of up to 6.7 km.

The torpedo system was of the usual configuration for Soviet destroyers of the period: a single five-tube MPTA-53-56M launcher for 533 mm torpedoes with the Stalingrad T-56 fire control system, which was fed data from the Zarya radar. The predominant torpedo was the type 53-56, which was able to reach a speed of 50 or 40 knots and a range of 8 or 13 km, respectively. The torpedo's warhead contained 400 kg of explosives. The armament was complemented by two 16-barrel RBU-2500 anti-submarine rocket launchers.

Complement

The ship was crewed by 266 men (later 268), including 20 officers. The officers were assigned cabins with two bunks each. The petty officers were split between three cabins, one each with 4, 6, or 8 bunks. The remainder of the crew slept in eight berth areas. These had, looking astern, 18, 24, 30, 30, 47, 48, 39, and 33 bunks stacked in three layers.

Flying the Polish Ensign

The *Spravedlivyy* arrived in Gdynia on 25 May 1970 and three days later the official transfer of the destroyer commenced. The naval ensign of Poland was hoisted on 25 June 1970, by which time the *Spravedlivyy* had already received her new name: ORP *Warszawa*. Thus, a tradition dating from before World War Two had been broken: that destroyers of the Polish Navy would be assigned names based on weather phenomena: *Burza* (storm), *Wicher* (gale), *Błyskawica* (lightning), etc. The vessel was also assigned the hull number 275, which she retained throughout her service in the Polish Navy. Initially, it was painted on both sides of the bow, later it appeared on the bridge wings. Commander Bogusław Gruchała became her first skipper.

After the destroyer had been commissioned in the Polish Navy, 29 Soviet instructors remained on the ship, including their commanding officer, Captain 2nd rank Ilya Birov. A purely Polish crew only began

Bow view.

manning the ship on 15 September 1970. Two months later, on 27 November, the ship fired her 130 mm guns for the first time and on 2 December launched her first SET-53 torpedoes against a submarine. The Soviet instructors left on 7 December 1970 the Soviet instructors left.

A warranty inspection of the ship was conducted in Baltiysk from 8–18 March 1971 after which she visited Baltiysk again on 25 May 1971. Three days later, at the Soviet rocket range, the Poles launched their first two V-601 SAMs. In 1971 the *Warszawa* spent 37 days at sea and covered 4,848 nautical miles. On 30 May she began her eight-day participation in the Baltic-72 exercise together with ships of the Soviet Baltic Fleet. In August 1973, during the Neptune-73 exercise, the destroyer fired the first anti-radar projectiles in the history of the Polish Navy: chaff rounds out of her main guns. In 1973 the *Warszawa* spent a record 111 days at sea.

The public was informed about the acquisition of the destroyer after a year had already passed! On 10 October 1971 the first class of Naval College students received their officer commissions and took their oaths on the *Warszawa*. In 1980, for the first time in the history of the Warsaw Pact armed forces, a joint naval squadron—modeled after NATO—was formed by the three member states with Baltic Sea coasts. The *Warszawa* joined the squadron alongside the Soviet *Kashin*-class destroyer *Slavnyy* and *Krivak*-class frigate *Neukrotimyy* as well as the East German *Koni*-class patrol ship *Rostock*. As part of the squadron the Polish destroyer crossed the North Sea all the way to the Shetland Islands. In 1983 she conducted a circumnavigation of the British Isles as part of the Eskadra-83 exercise, taking on fuel from the Soviet tanker *Lena*, and in 1984 she made a port call in Murmansk. In 1985 she participated in exercises for the last time.

During her service in the Polish Navy, the *Warszawa* made port calls in Leningrad, USSR (1972, 1976, 1981, 1985), Helsinki, Finland (1972. 1980), Le Havre, France (1973), Portsmouth, UK (1975), London, UK (1977), Copenhagen, Denmark (1978), Karlskrona, Sweden (1978), and Murmansk, USSR (1984).

During the 15 years of flying the Polish ensign she covered 77,392 nautical miles. On 31 January 1986 the flag was lowered for the last time. In 1991 the *Warszawa* was towed to Świnoujście and scrapped by a private company.

Stern view.

Chronology

Entered into the Soviet Naval Vessel Register: 15 September 1953
Laid down: 25 December 1954 (construction number 709)
Launched: 12 April 1956
Completed: 20 December 1956
Commissioned: 27 December 1956
Transferred to the Polish Navy: 25 June 1970
Struck from the Soviet Naval Vessel Register: 27 January 1971
Armament removed and struck from the Polish Navy: 1 January 1986

The Polish commanders of ORP *Warszawa*

Kpt. mar. (CDR) Bogusław Gruchała (25.06.1970 – 23.02.1972)
Kpt. mar. Edmund Chełchowski (23.02.1972 – 27.08.1976)
Kpt. mar. Jerzy Wójcik (27.08.1976 – 31.01.1986)

Bibliography

Y.V. Apalkov, Jesmincy proektov 56, 57 bis i ih modifikacii, Moskva 2009.
S.S. Berezhnoj, Krejsera i minonoscy, Moskva 2002.
Koszela W., Niszczyciele Polskiej Marynarki Wojennej. Warszawa 2013.
A.S. Pavlov, Jeskadrennye minonoscy proekta 56, Yakutsk 1999.
A.V. Platonov, Sovetskie minonoscy. Chast' 2, Petersburg 2003.
R. Rochowicz, Niszczyciele projektu 56K/A/AE. Nowa Technika Wojskowa 12/1996.
R. Rochowicz, Rakietowa „stolica" ORP Warszawa (I). Morza Statki i Okręty 5/2000.
R. Rochowicz, Dzieje niszczyciela ORP Warszawa, „Morze Statki i Okręty" 1/2015.
V.P. Zablockij, Pod imenem Kotlin, Ocherki voenno-morskoj istorii, No. 7.
V.P. Zablockij, Pod imenem Kotlin, Ocherki voenno-morskoj istorii, No. 8.

Bow port of the ship with SM-2-1 130 mm gun mount.

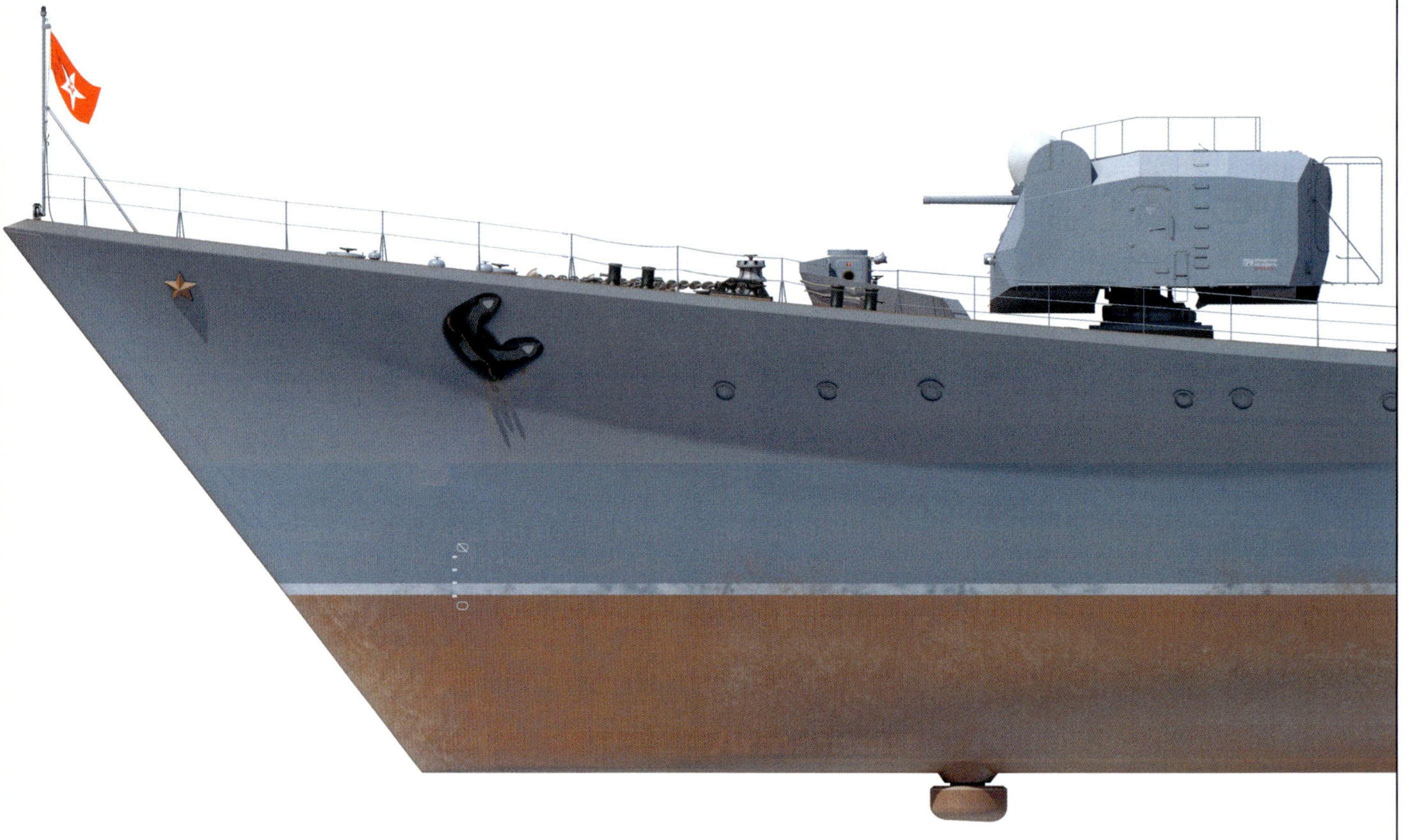

Bow superstructure with FUT-B radar antenna.

Starboard view on the bow superstructure; quad SM-20 ZIF 45 mm gun mount in front.

Port side view on the superstructure; FUT-B radar antenna and SWP-42-50 homing post with Jakor-M radar antenna on the roof.

Port side of the midship with the bow PTA-53-56 533 mm torpedo launcher battery; anti-rolling fin below the waterline.

Midship with a stern funnel and quad SM-20-ZIF 45 mm gun mount on the starboard.

Main mast with Rif radar antenna; behind on the lower platform Fut-B radar antenna.

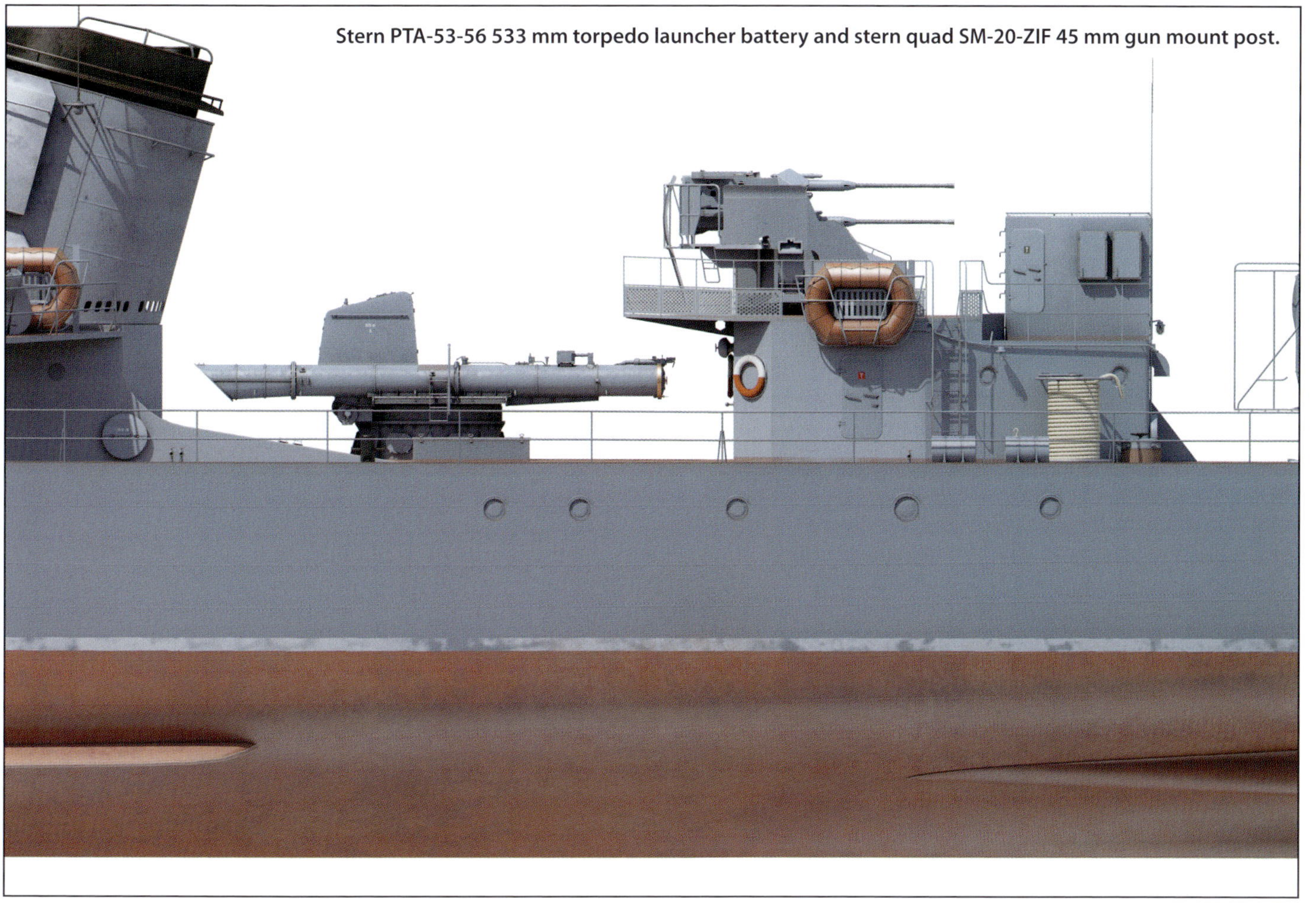

Stern PTA-53-56 533 mm torpedo launcher battery and stern quad SM-20-ZIF 45 mm gun mount post.

Port side view; container with prepared ammunition in front of SM-20-ZIF gun mount.

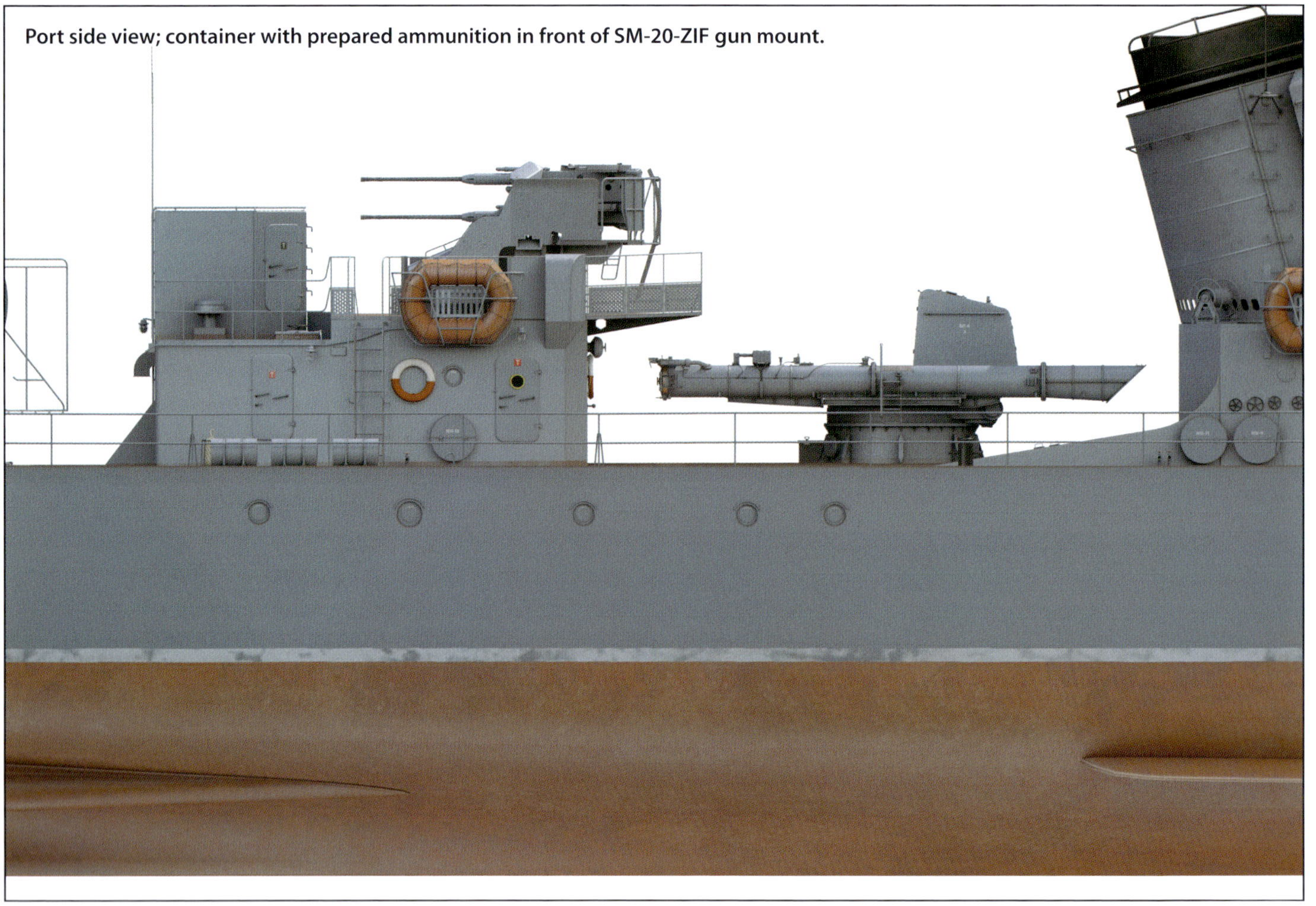

Bow SM-2-1 130 mm gun mount.

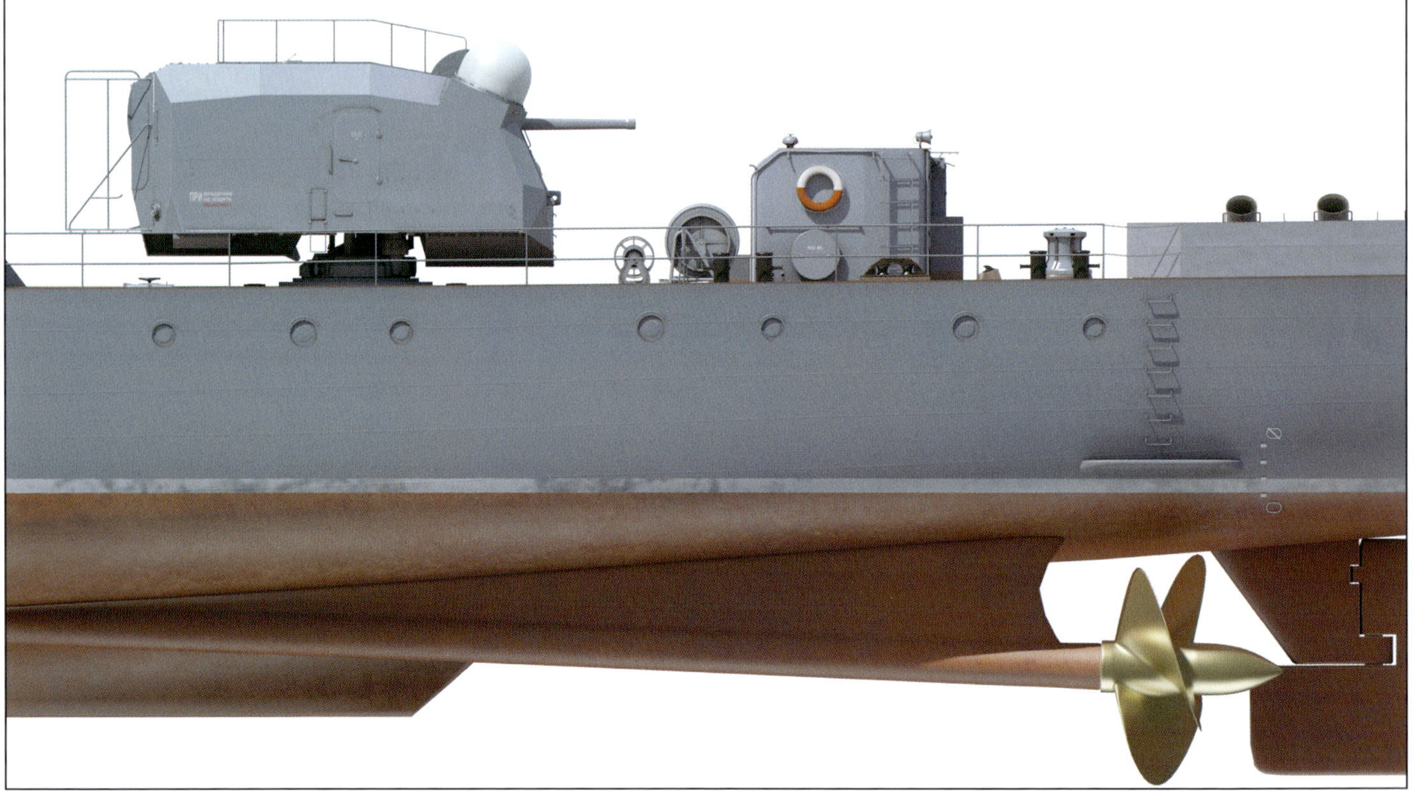

Port bow view; left propeller and ship's wheel.

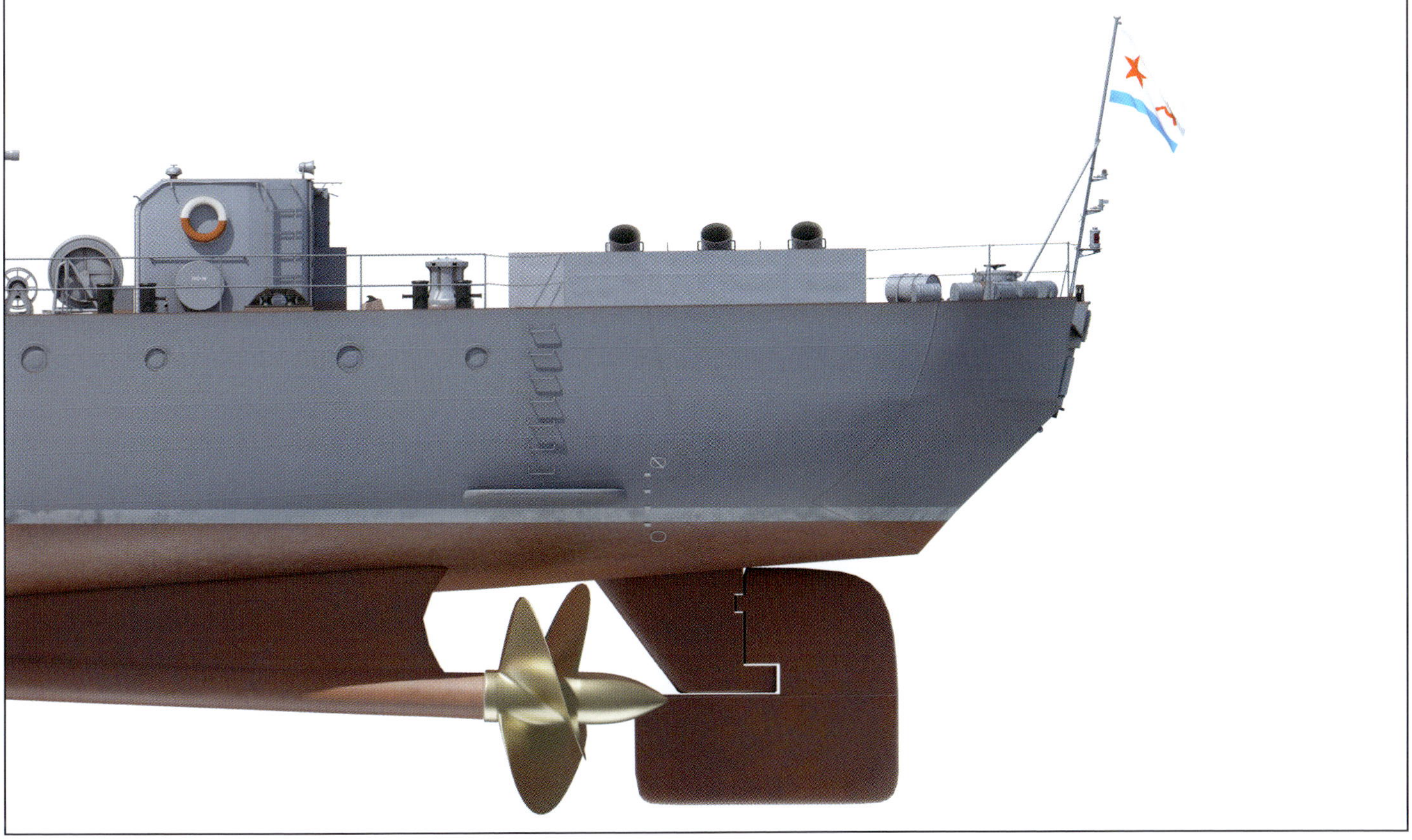

Starboard stern view; right propeller and ship's wheel.

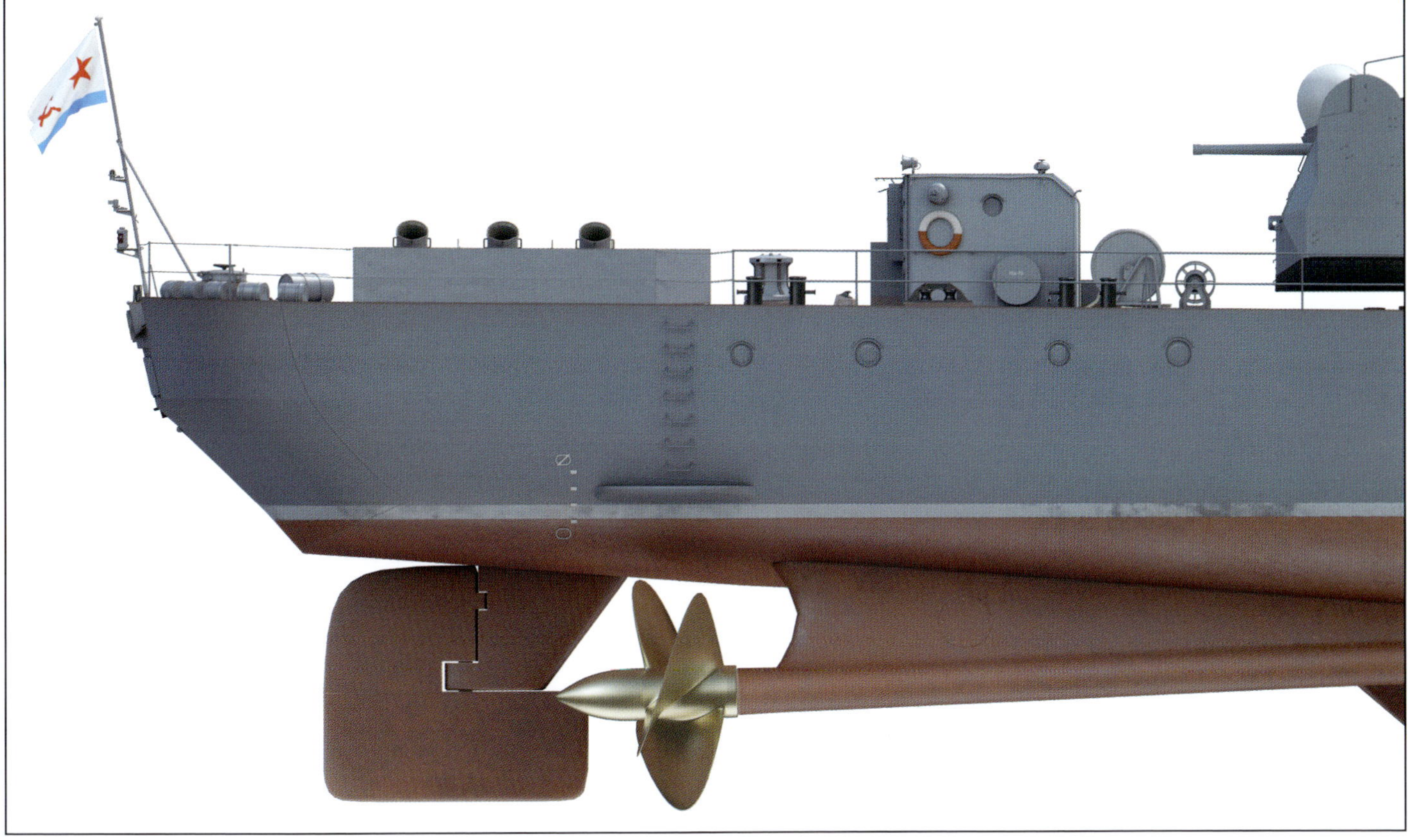

Top view on the stern; BMB-2 depth charge throwers and depth charge racks.

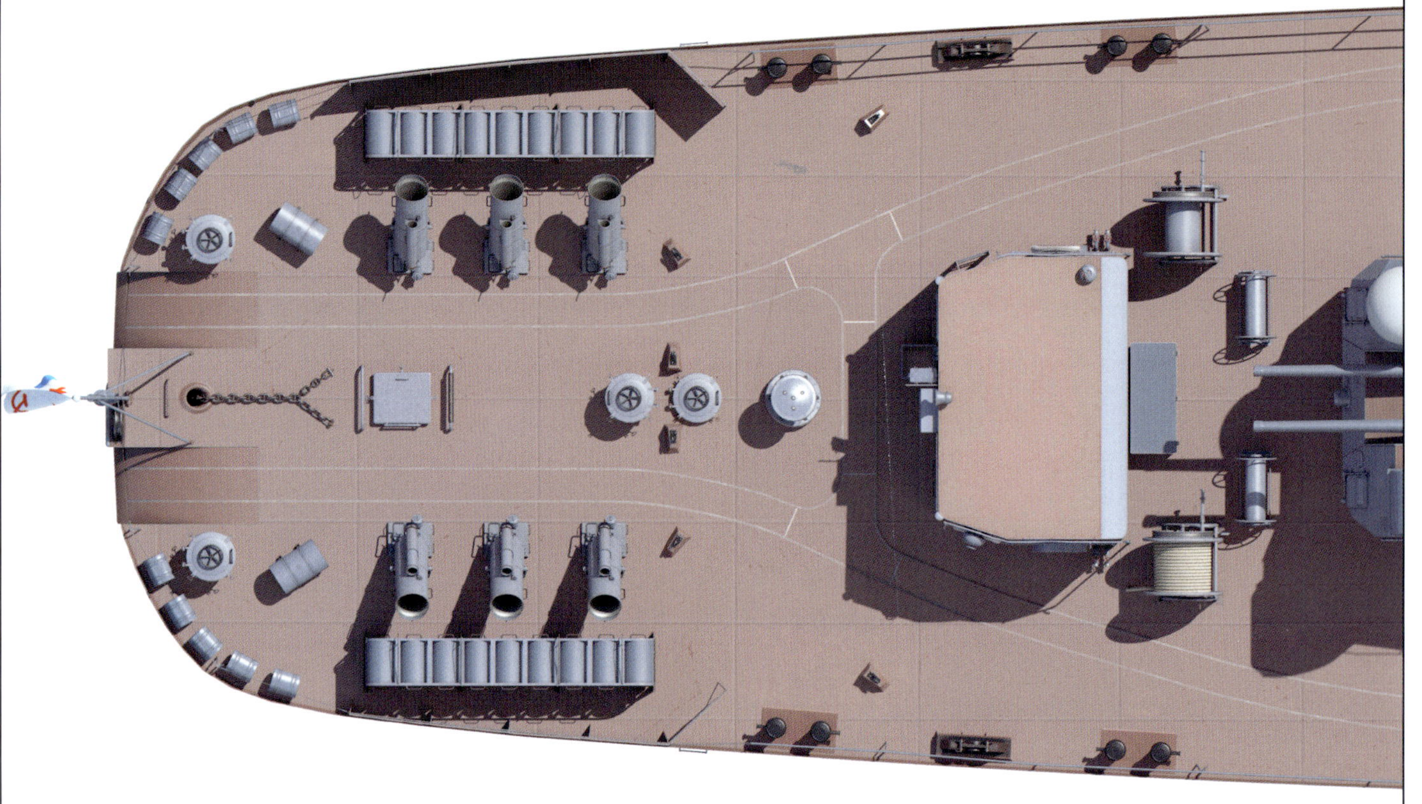

Top view on the stern SM-2-1 130 mm gun mount.

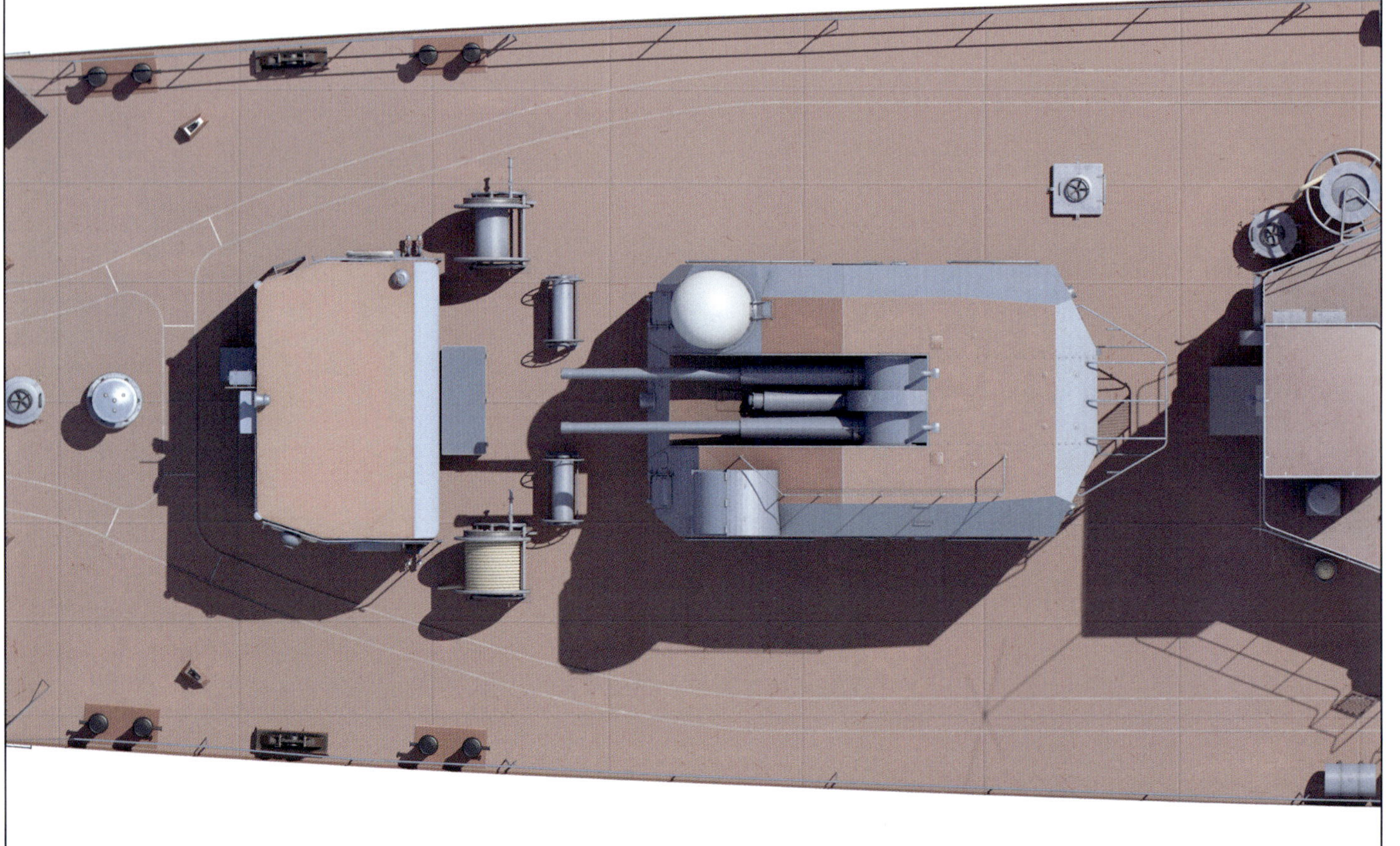

Top view on the stern PTA-53-56 torpedo launcher battery and stern SM-20-ZIF post.

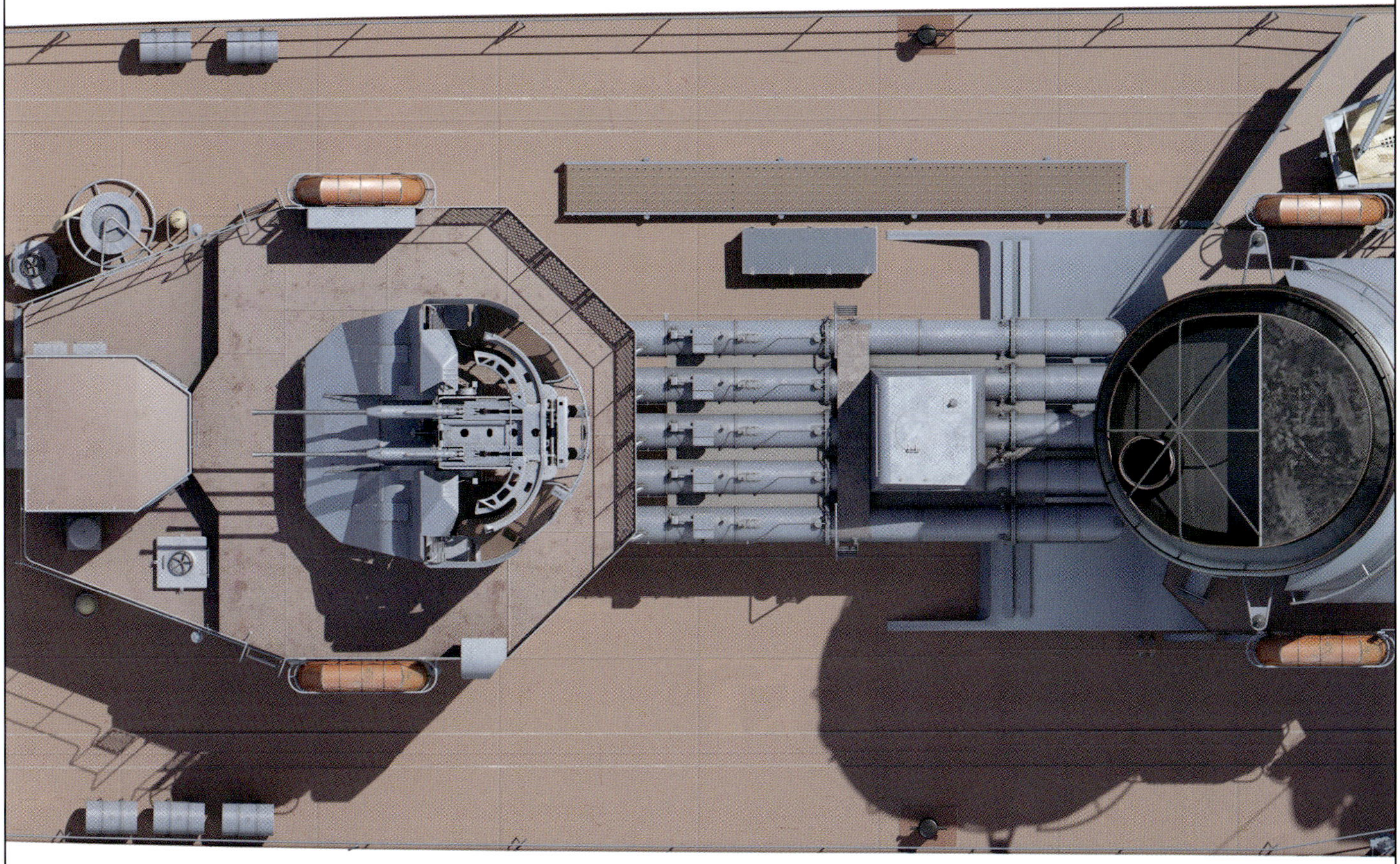

Top view on the bow PTA-53-56 torpedo launcher battery and two side SM-20-ZIF posts.

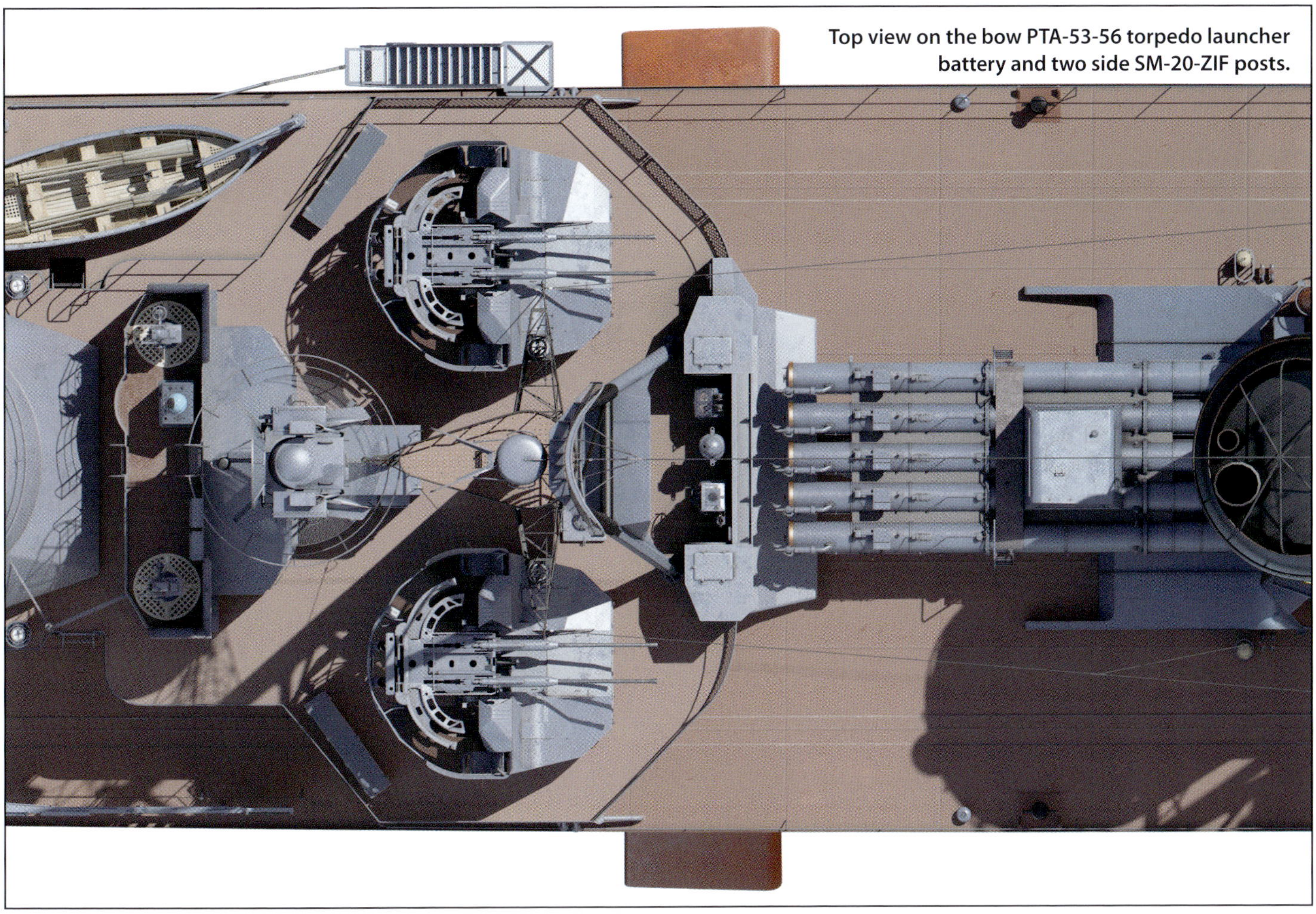

Top view on the captain's bridge and bow funnel.

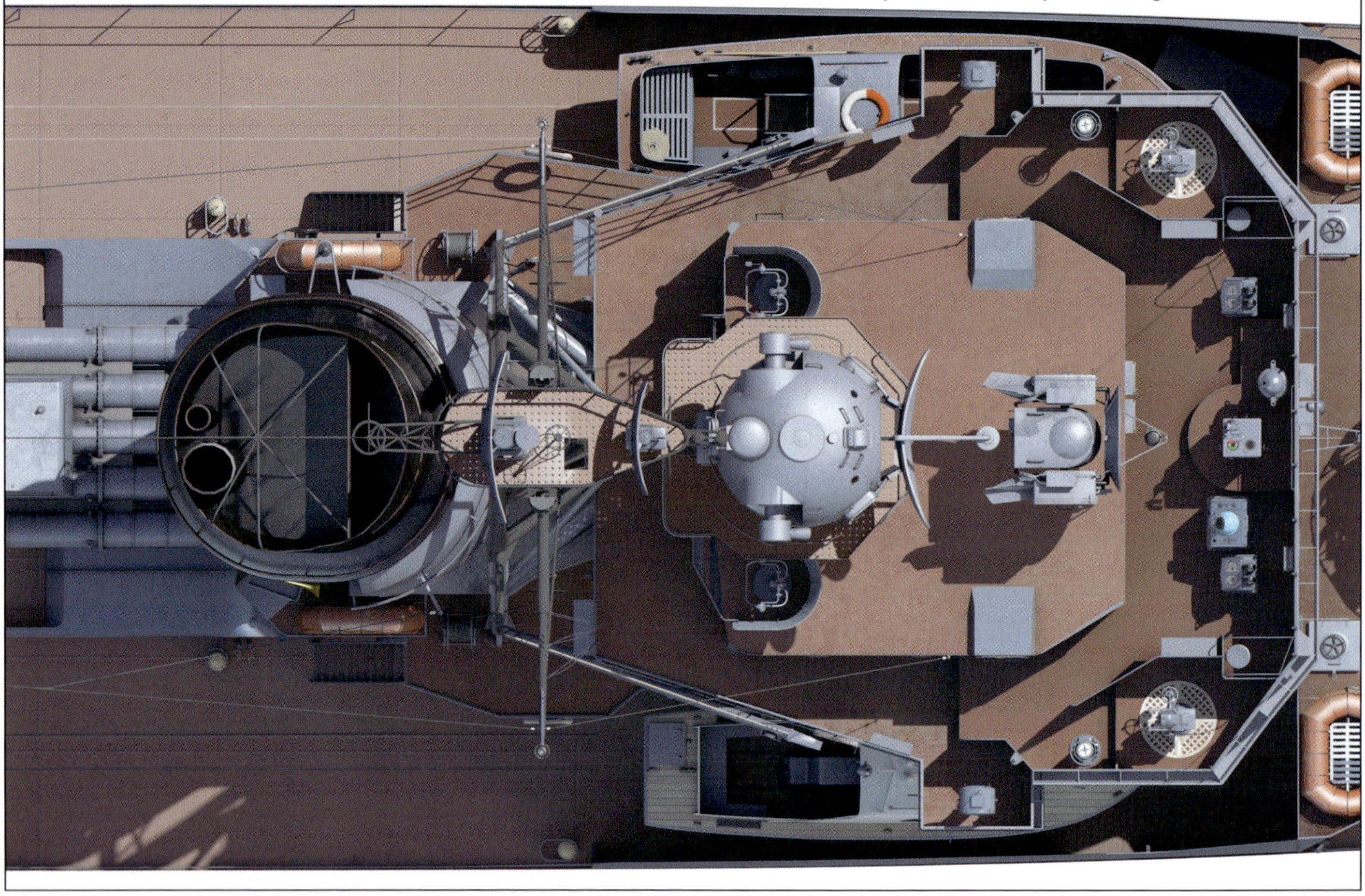

Top view on the bow SM-2-1 130 mm gun mount and SM-20-ZIF post.

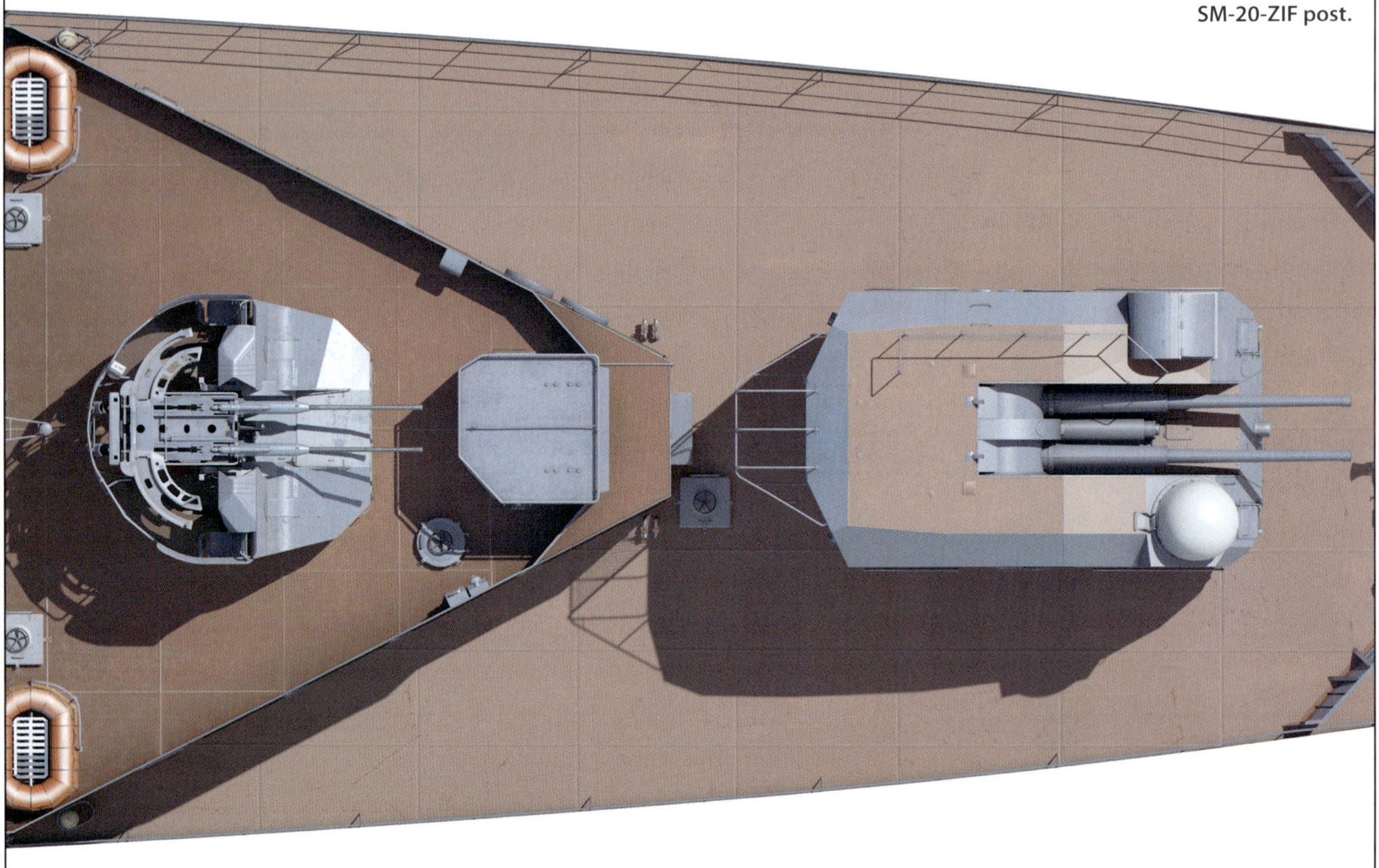

Top view on the bow; breakwater, capstans, and anchor chains visible.

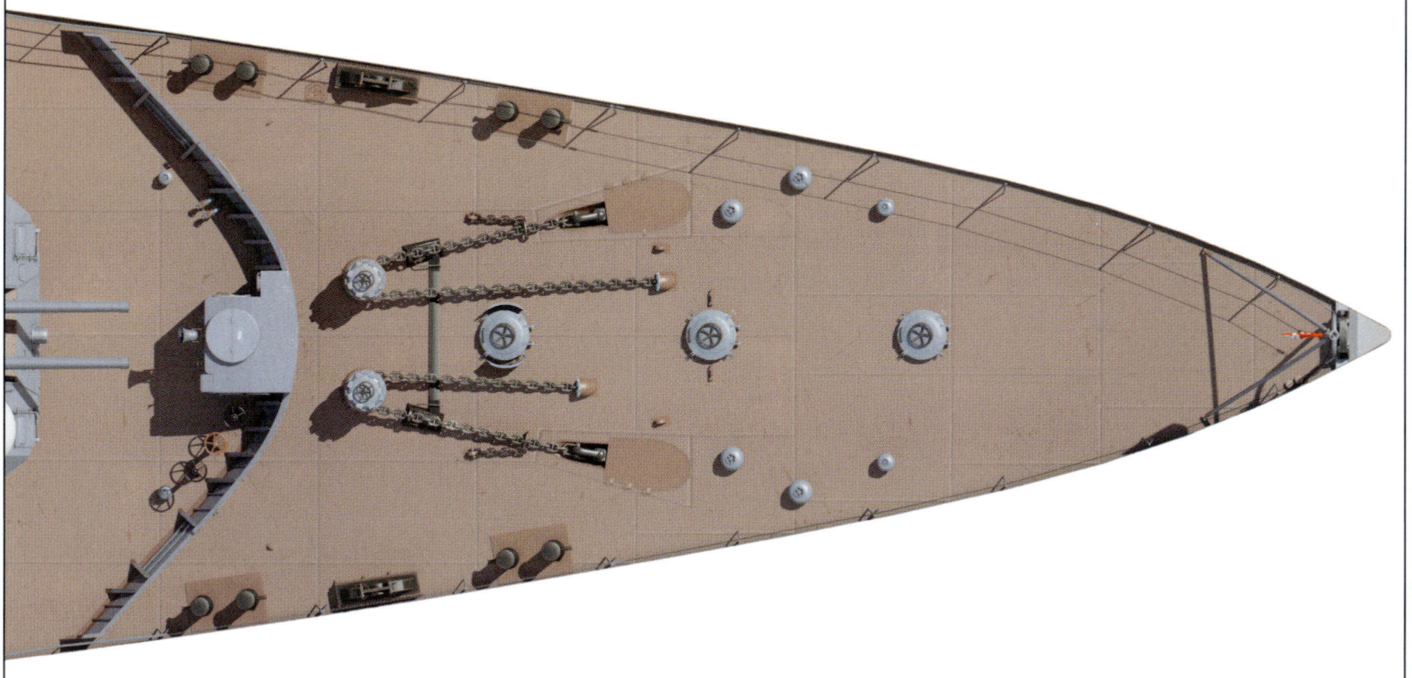

Port bow view; staff with the USSR Navy jack.

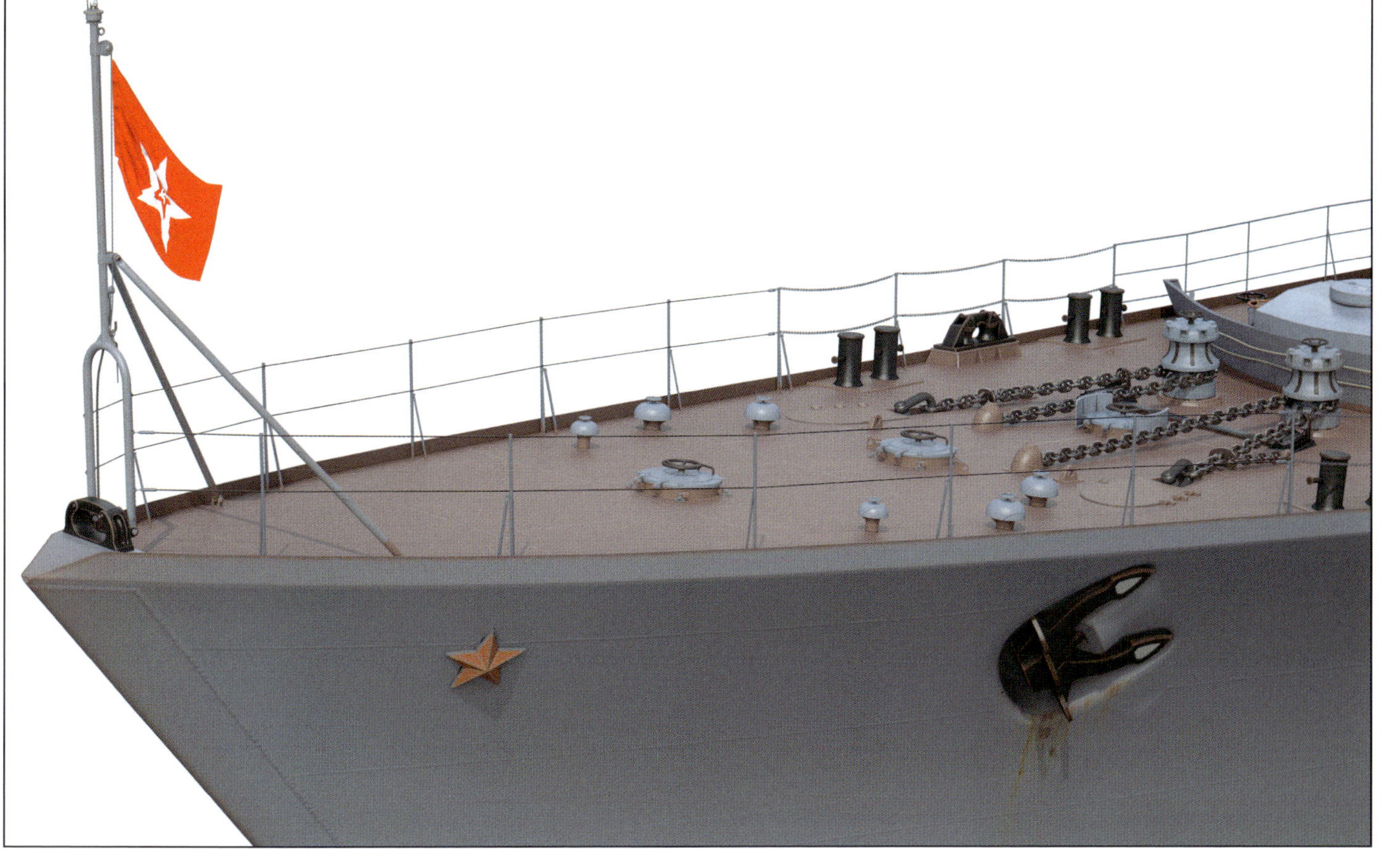

Bow view on SM-2-1 gun mount and the captain's bridge.

Bow SM-2-1 130 mm gun mount with Sztag-B radar distance finder (in white dome).

Capstans and anchor chains.

Port-side part of the breakwater; inside a companionway to the crew's forecastle.

Starboard part of the breakwater.

Left side of the SM-2-1 gun mount.

Right side of the bow superstructure with the command bridge and SM-20-ZIF post.

Bow SM-20-ZIF gun mount post.

Port side view of the bridge on the rear of SM-2-1 gun mount.

Superstructure with containers with prepared 45 mm ammunition and elevators.

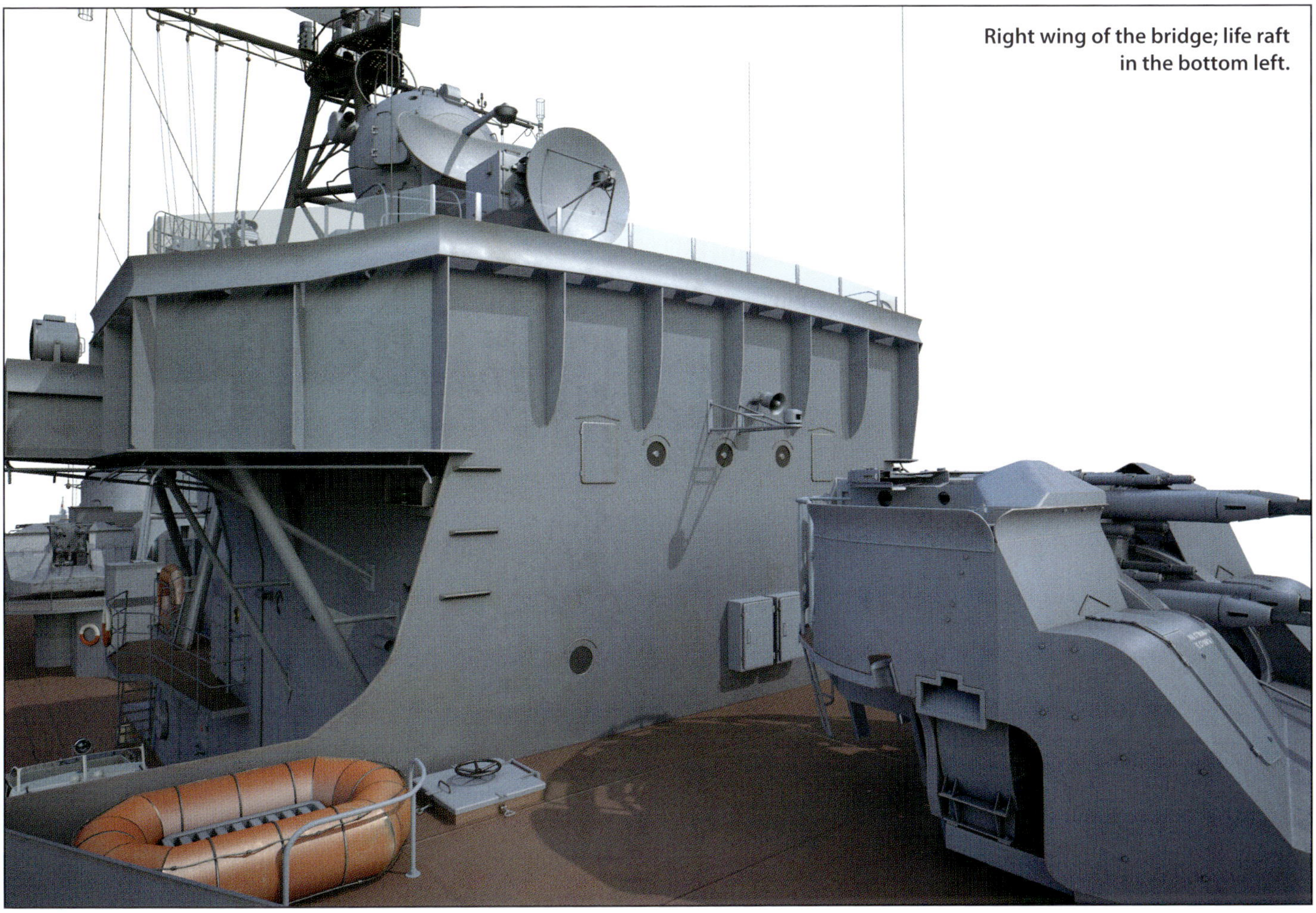

Right wing of the bridge; life raft in the bottom left.

Starboard navigation light (green).

Bridge windscreen, further FUT-B radar antenna and SWP-42-50 homing post with Jakor-M radar antenna

Right wing of the bridge with WCUZ-3 optical sight.

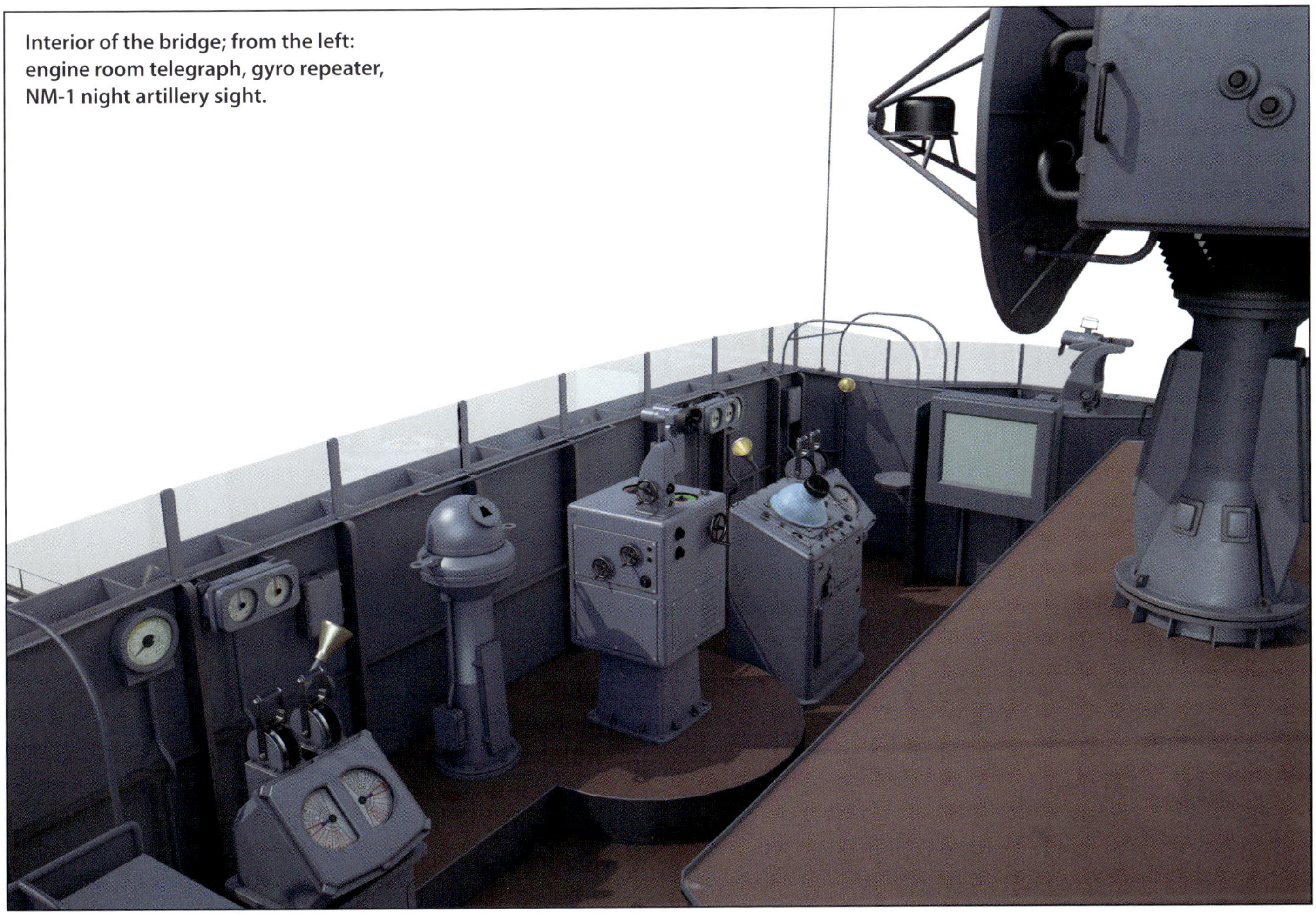

Interior of the bridge; from the left: engine room telegraph, gyro repeater, NM-1 night artillery sight.

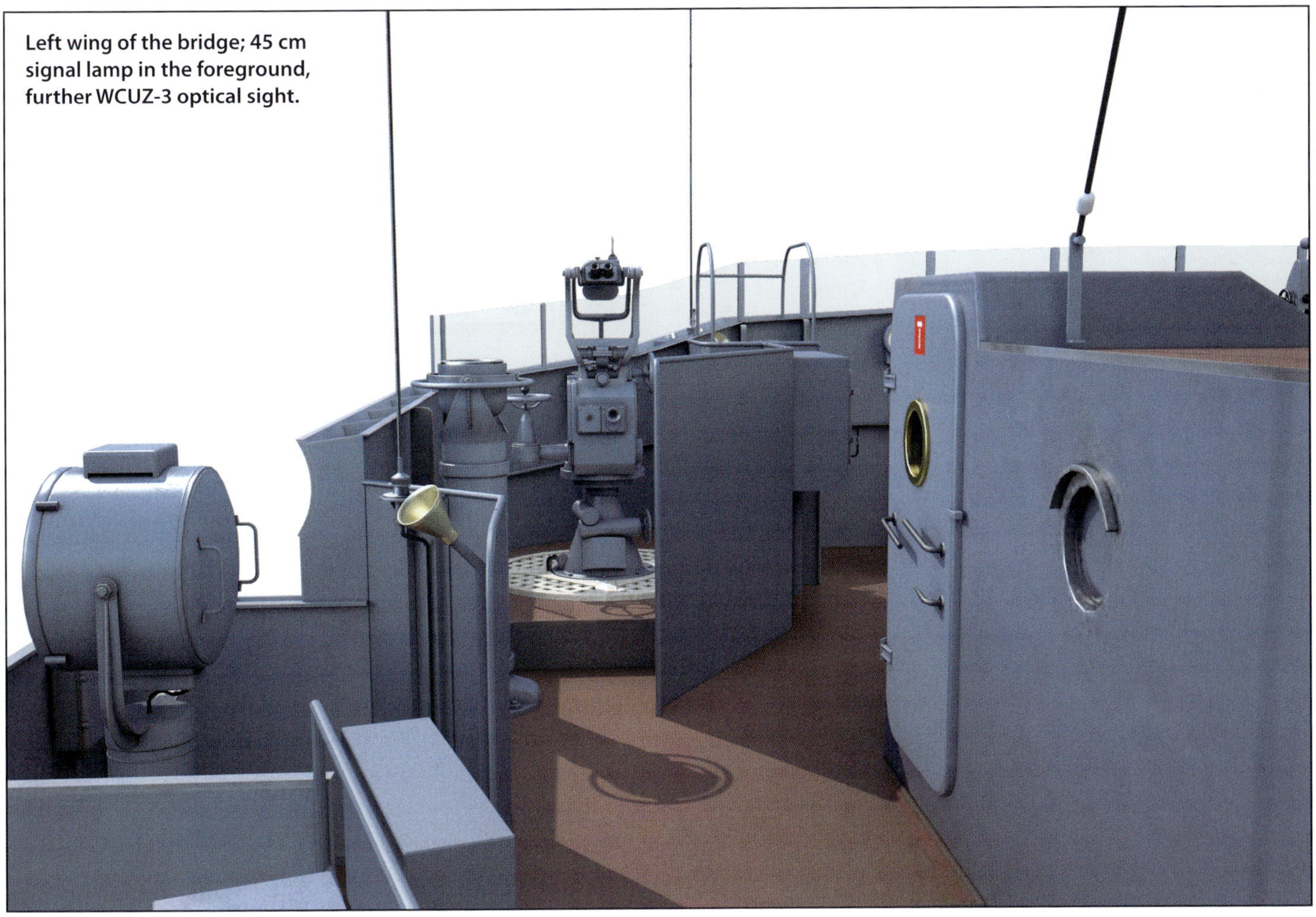

Left wing of the bridge; 45 cm signal lamp in the foreground, further WCUZ-3 optical sight.

Bridge equipment; from the left: engine room telegraph, gyro repeater, NM-1 night artillery sight.

Bridge interior; emergency engine room telegraph on the right.

Left wing of the bridge with a 45 cm signal lamp.

Part of the motor launch boom (port side).

Part of the motor launch boom (starboard).

Fut-B radar antenna.

SWP-42-50 post barbette.

SM-20-ZIF 45 mm battery commander's post.

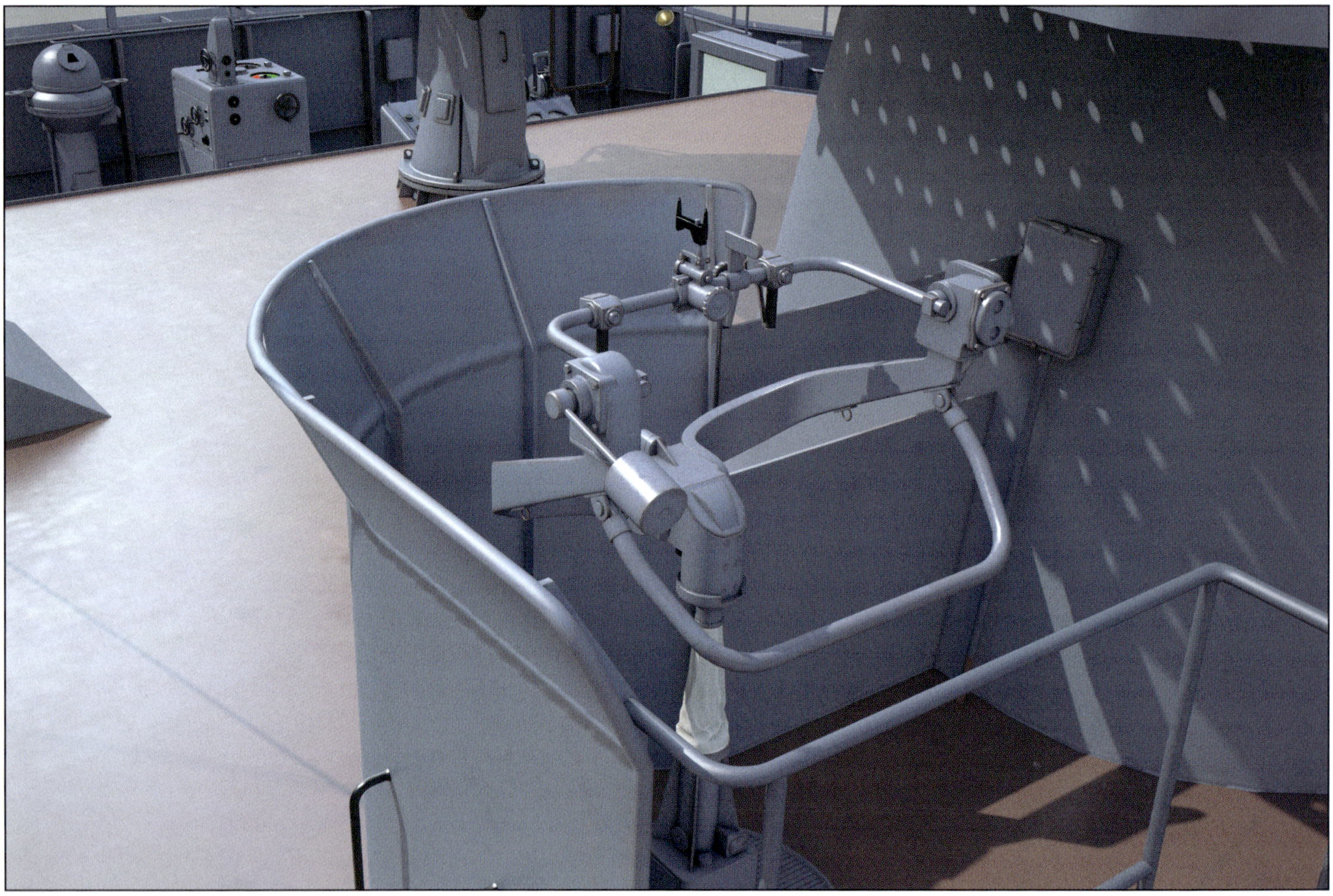

Battery commander's 15-A instrument.

SWP-42-50 post barbette.

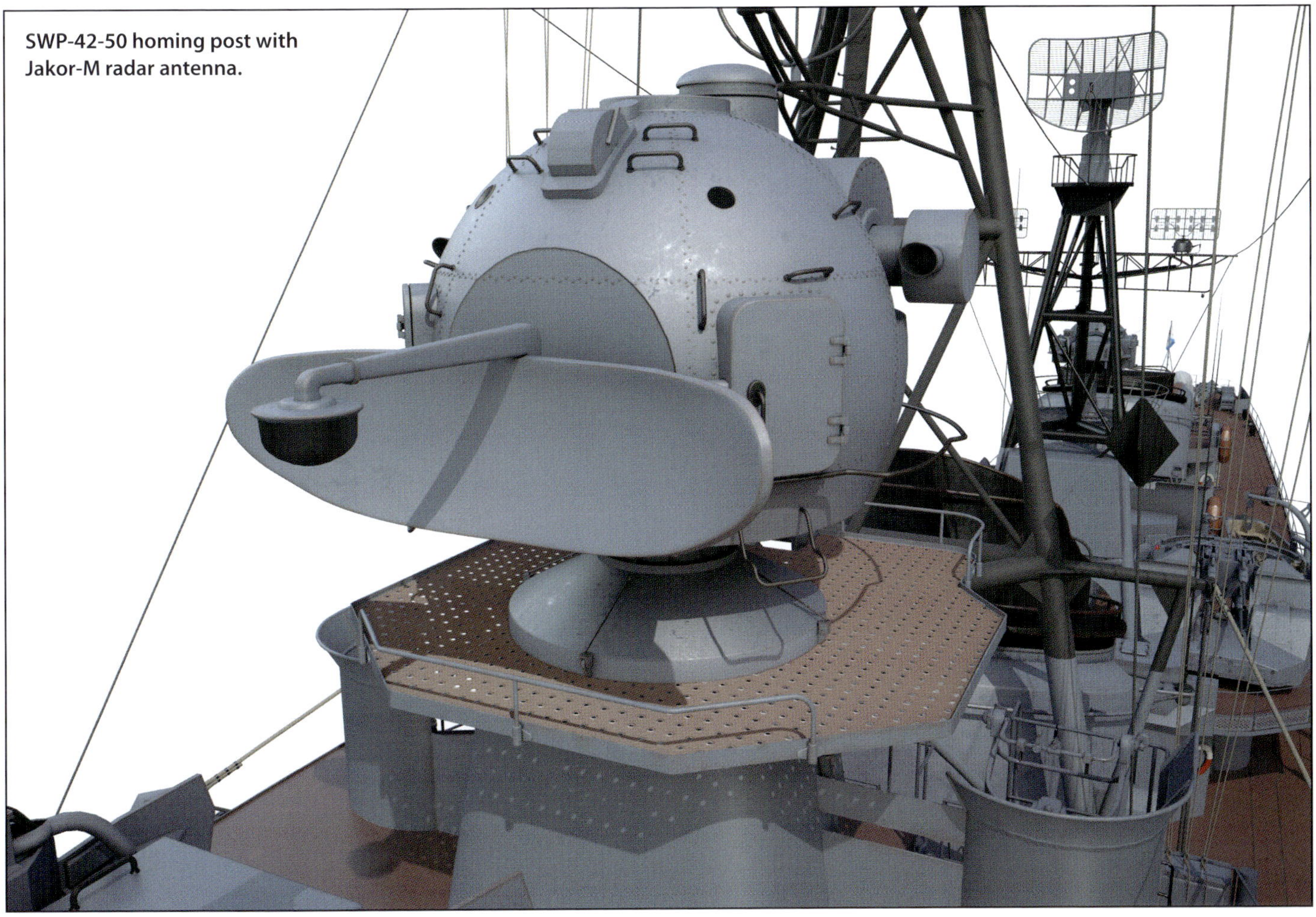

SWP-42-50 homing post with Jakor-M radar antenna.

Side view of SWP-42-50.

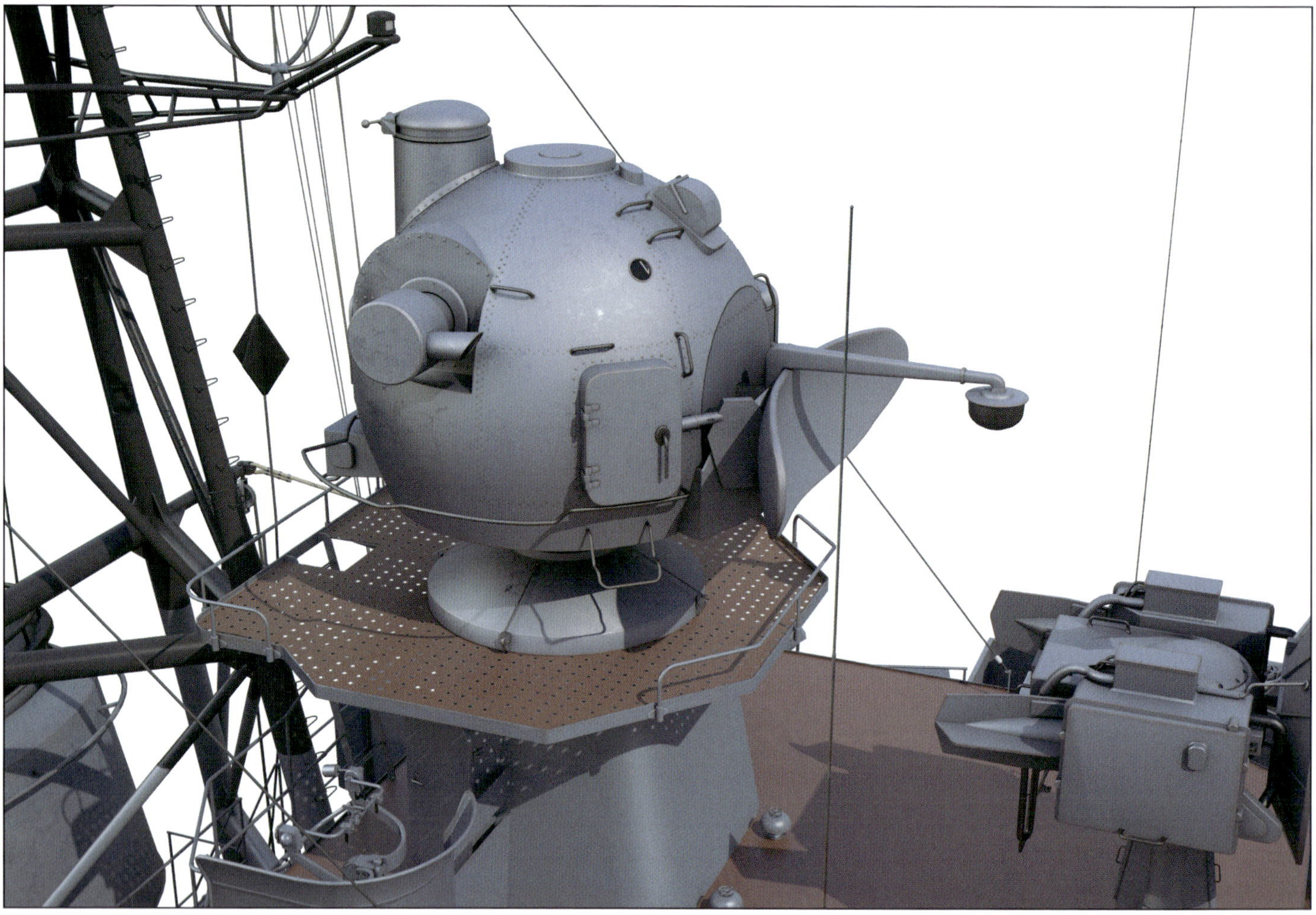

Another views of SWP-42-50.

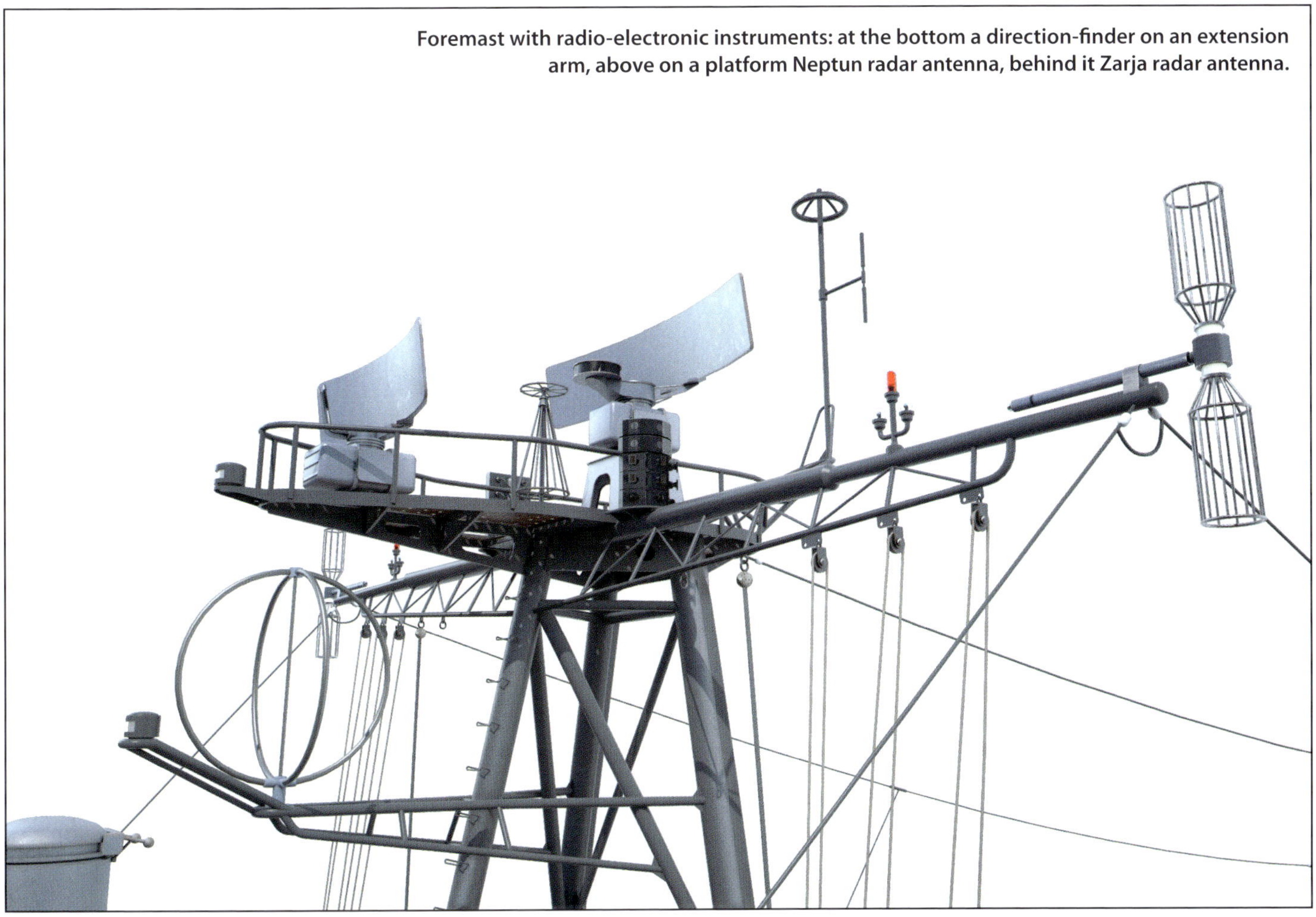

Foremast with radio-electronic instruments: at the bottom a direction-finder on an extension arm, above on a platform Neptun radar antenna, behind it Zarja radar antenna.

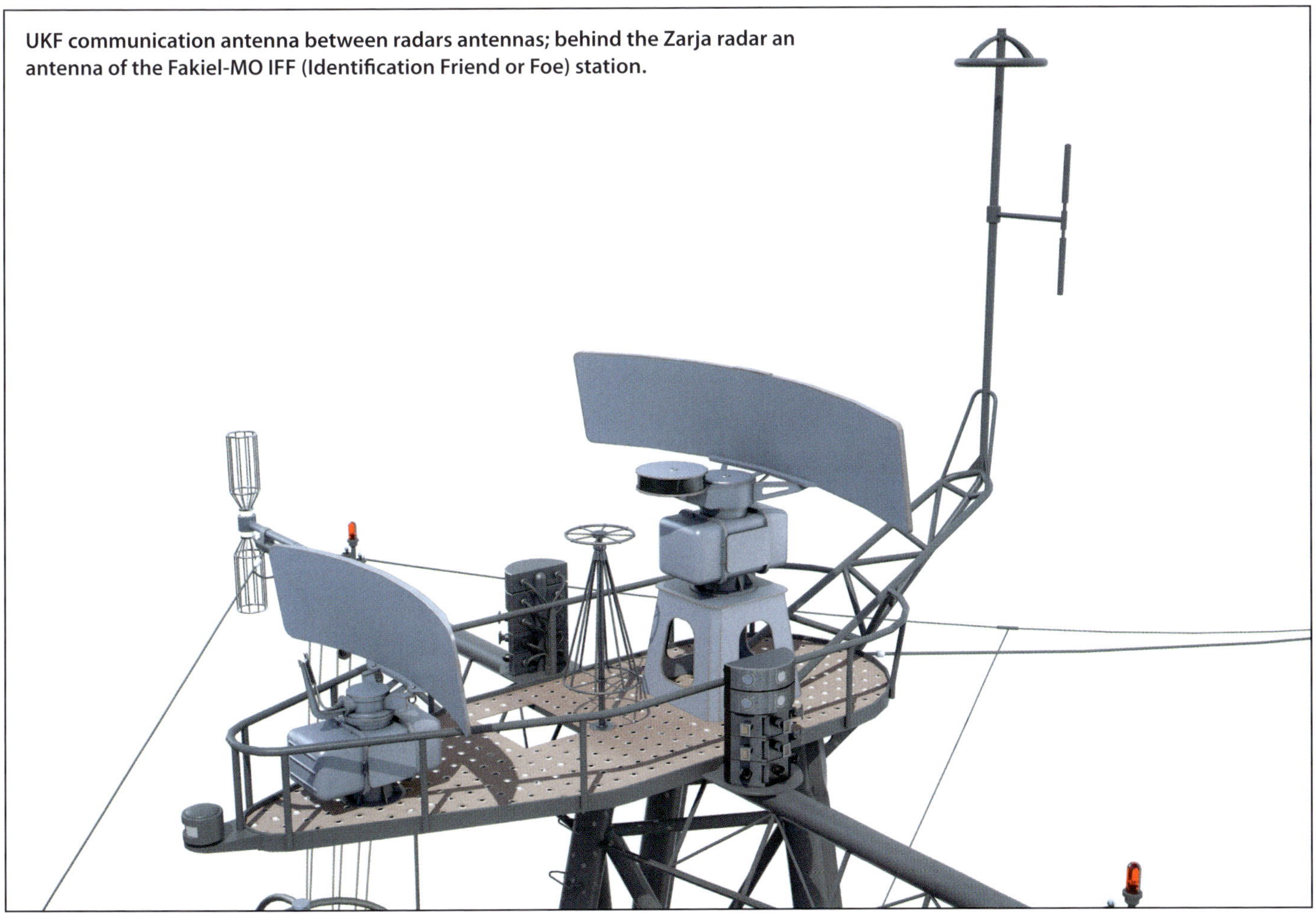

UKF communication antenna between radars antennas; behind the Zarja radar an antenna of the Fakiel-MO IFF (Identification Friend or Foe) station.

Antenna of the Neptun navigation radar.

Ribbed back of the Neptun radar antenna.

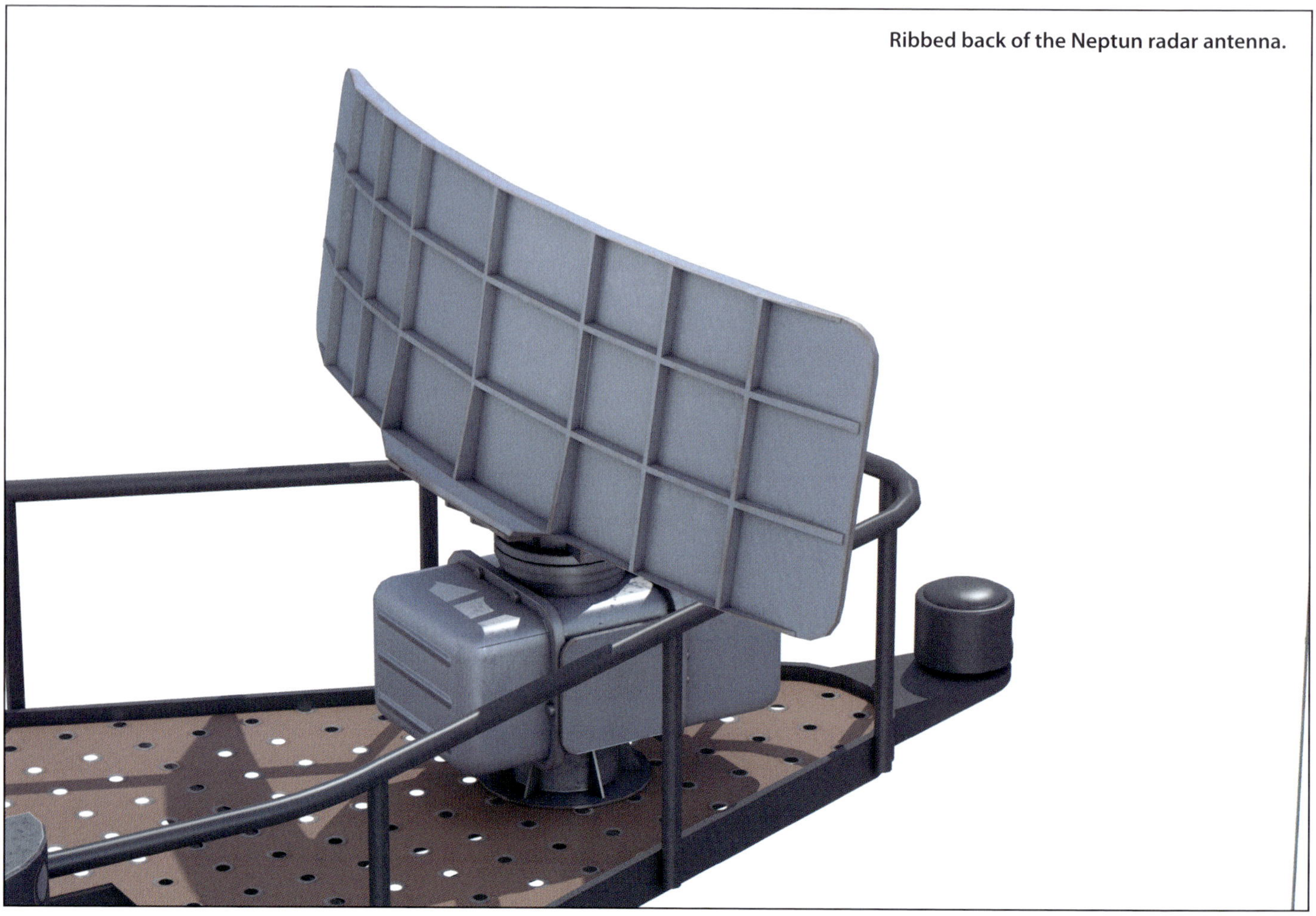

Antenna of the Zarja torpedo fire-control radar.

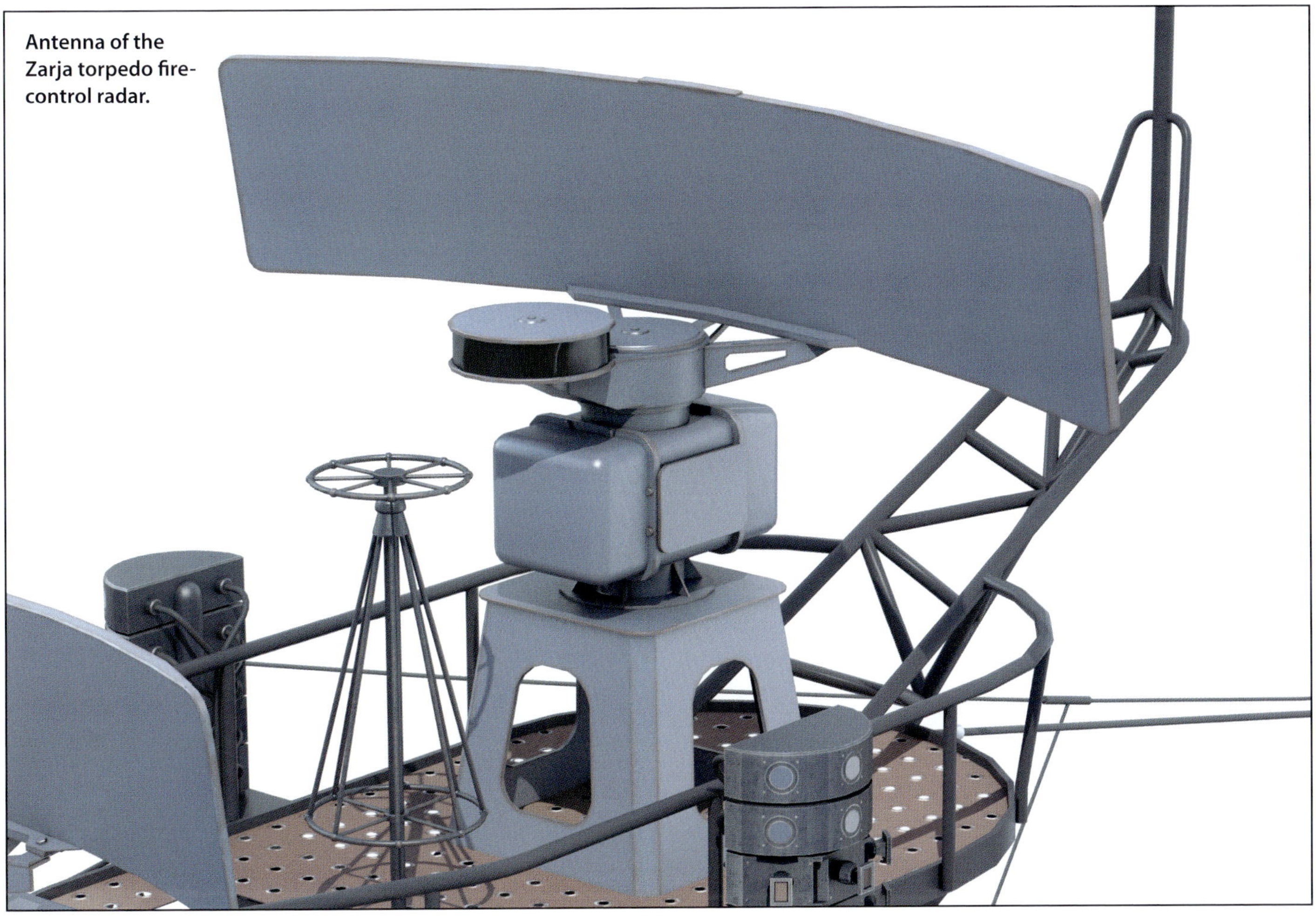

Ribbed back of the Zarja radar antenna, UKF communication antenna on the left.

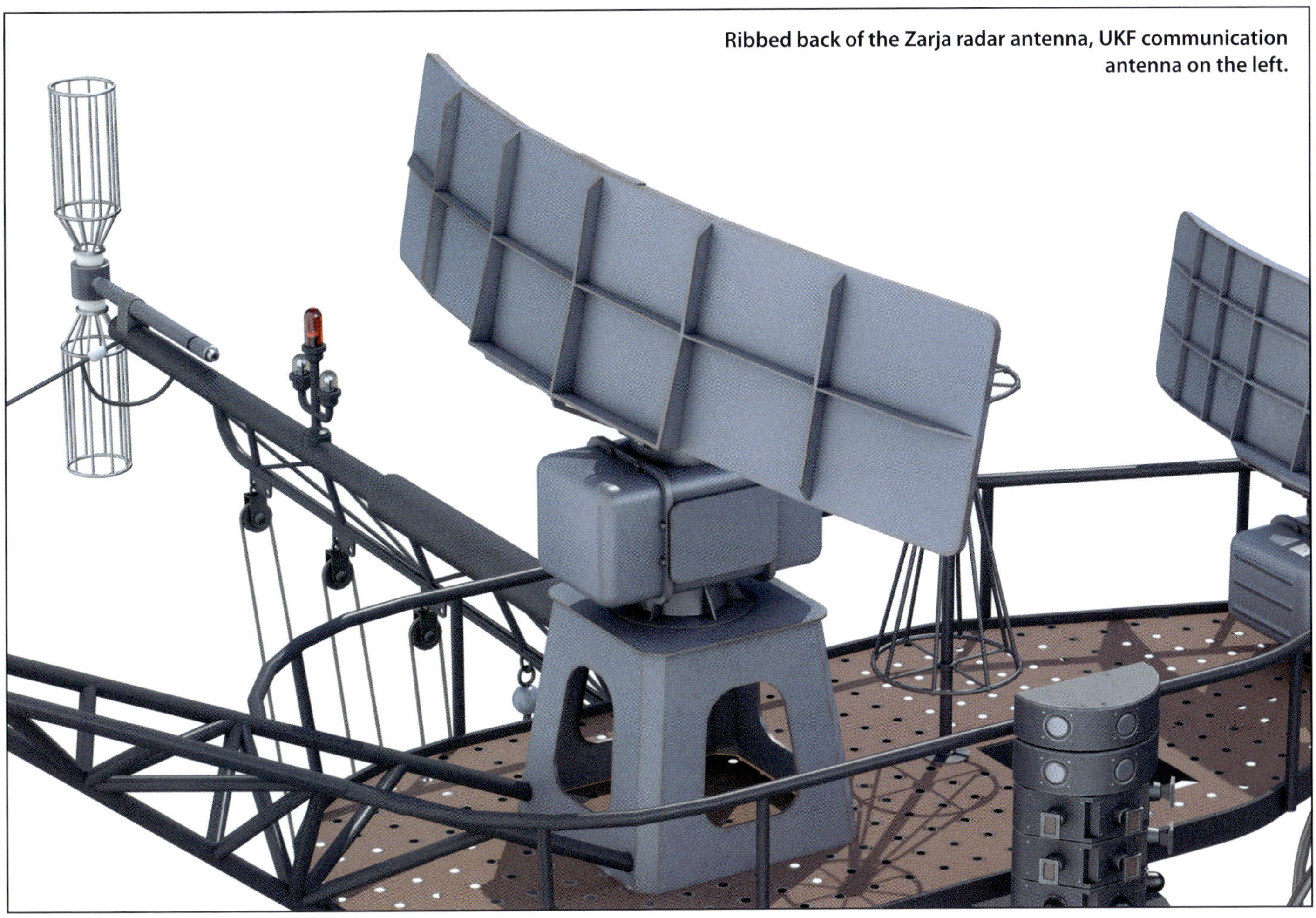

Maczta-P radiotechnical reconnaissance station.

Boat of the ship commander.

Cover of the bow funnel; life raft on the side; front door to the washroom on the right.

Port side, bow of the work boat (motor launch).

Port side; stern of the work boat visible on the left side; cover of the bow funnel in the middle; life raft on the side.

Bow funnel and boom to operate the work boat.

Port side; SWP-42-50 post barbette, tripod foremast and bow funnel.

Cover of the bow funnel with smoke flues.

Stern view on the bow funnel and bow superstructure; boat of the ship commander visible on the right.

Bow PTA 53-56 torpedo launcher battery.

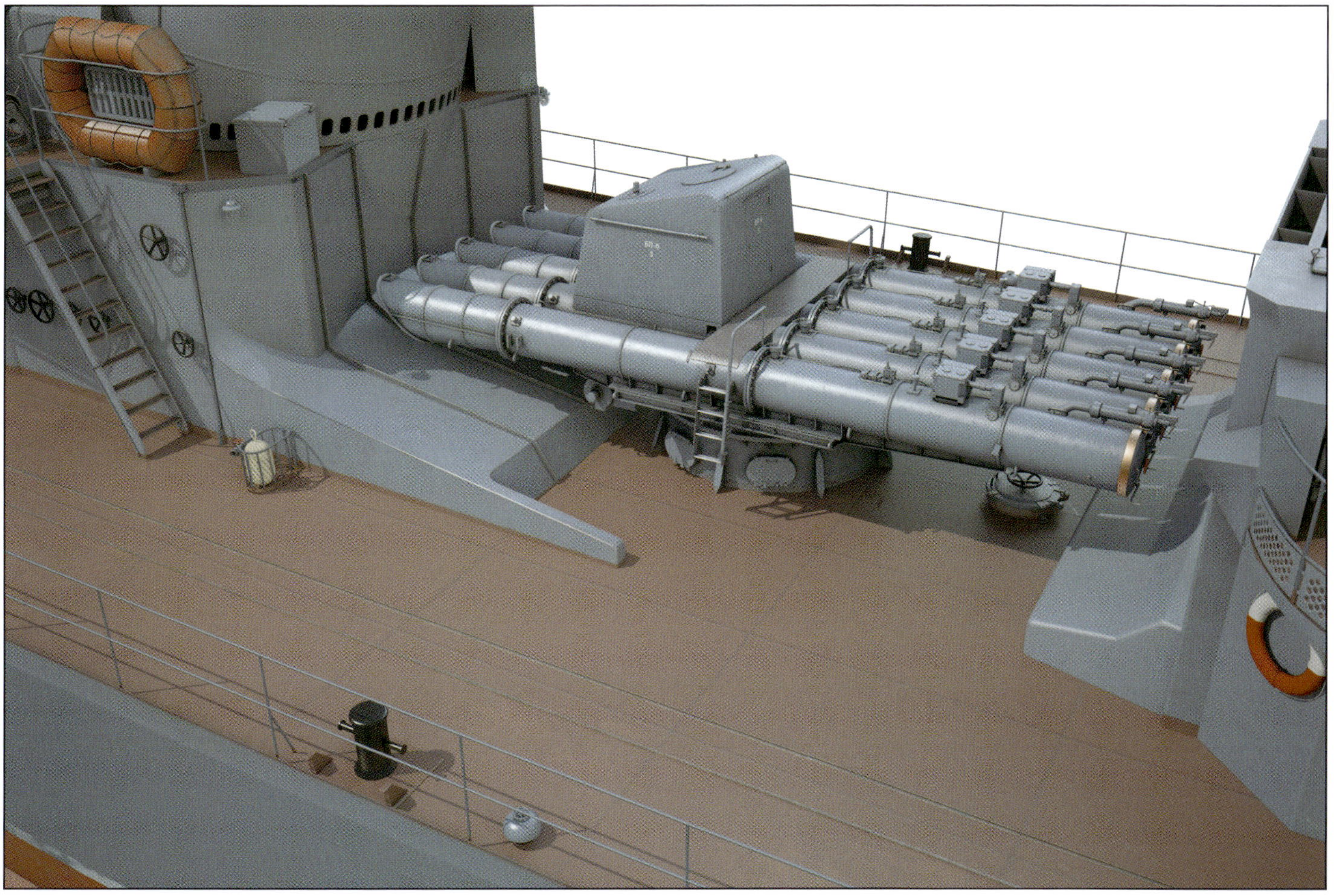

The same PTA 53-56 torpedo launcher battery (port side view).

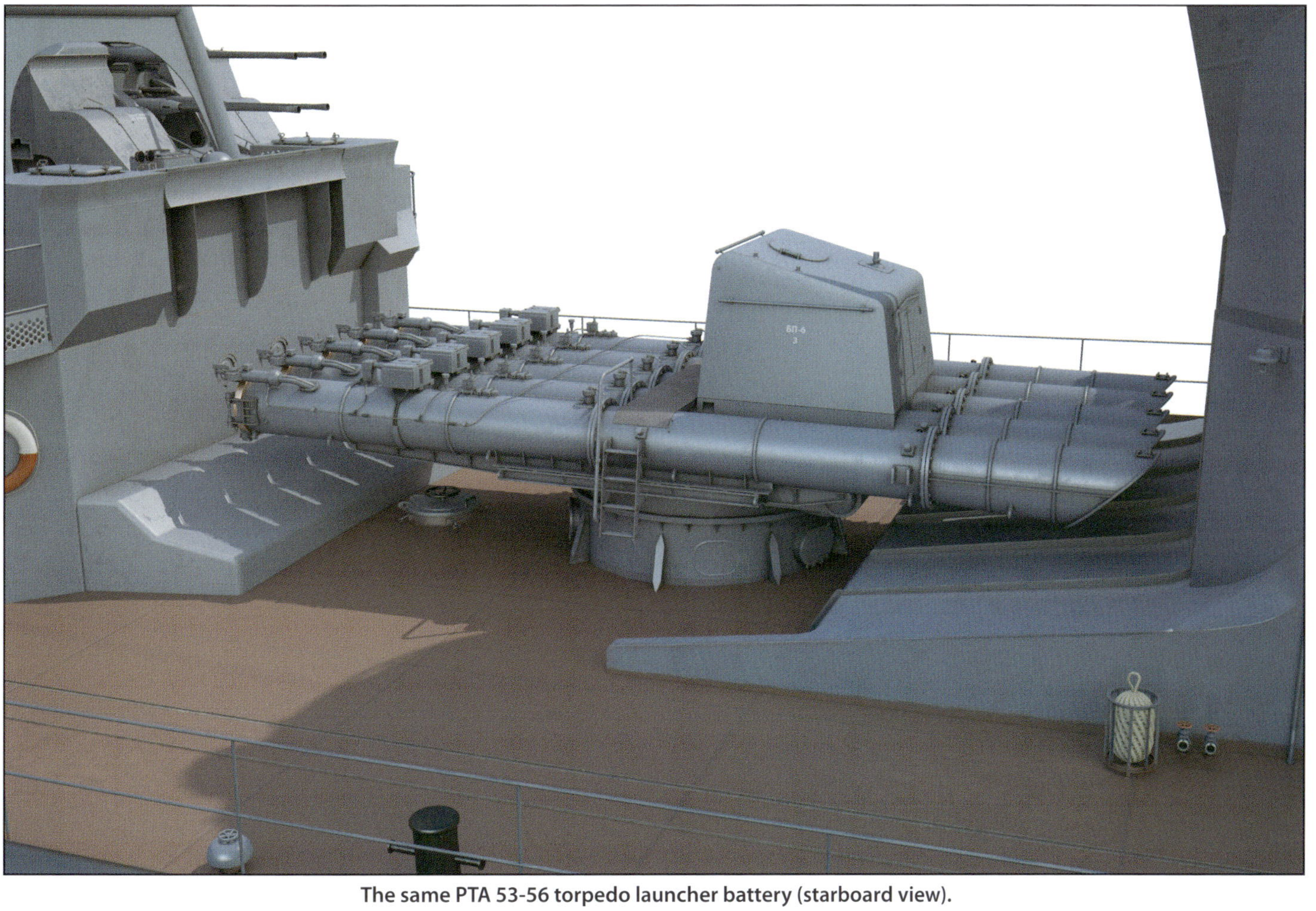

The same PTA 53-56 torpedo launcher battery (starboard view).

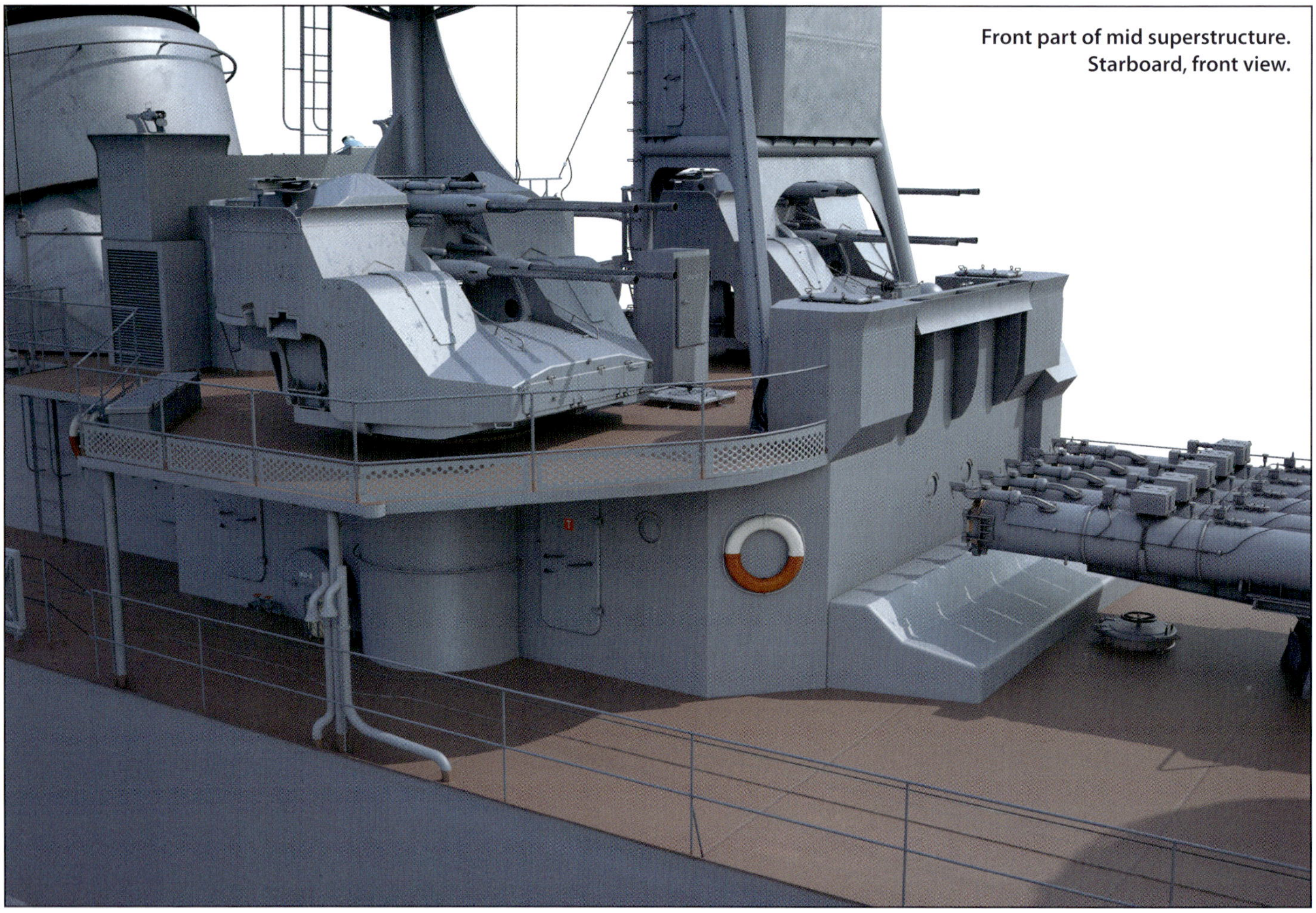
Front part of mid superstructure.
Starboard, front view.

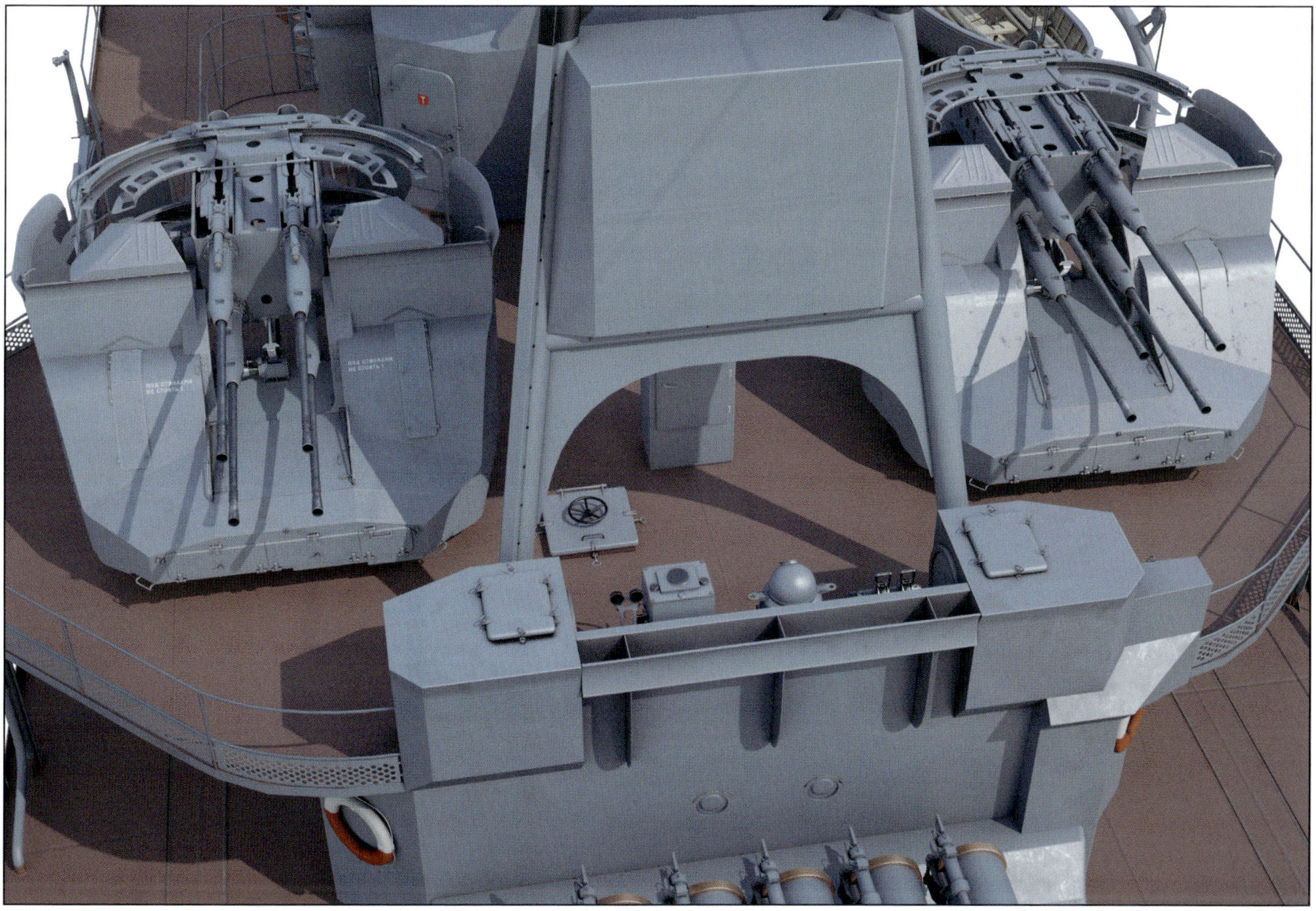

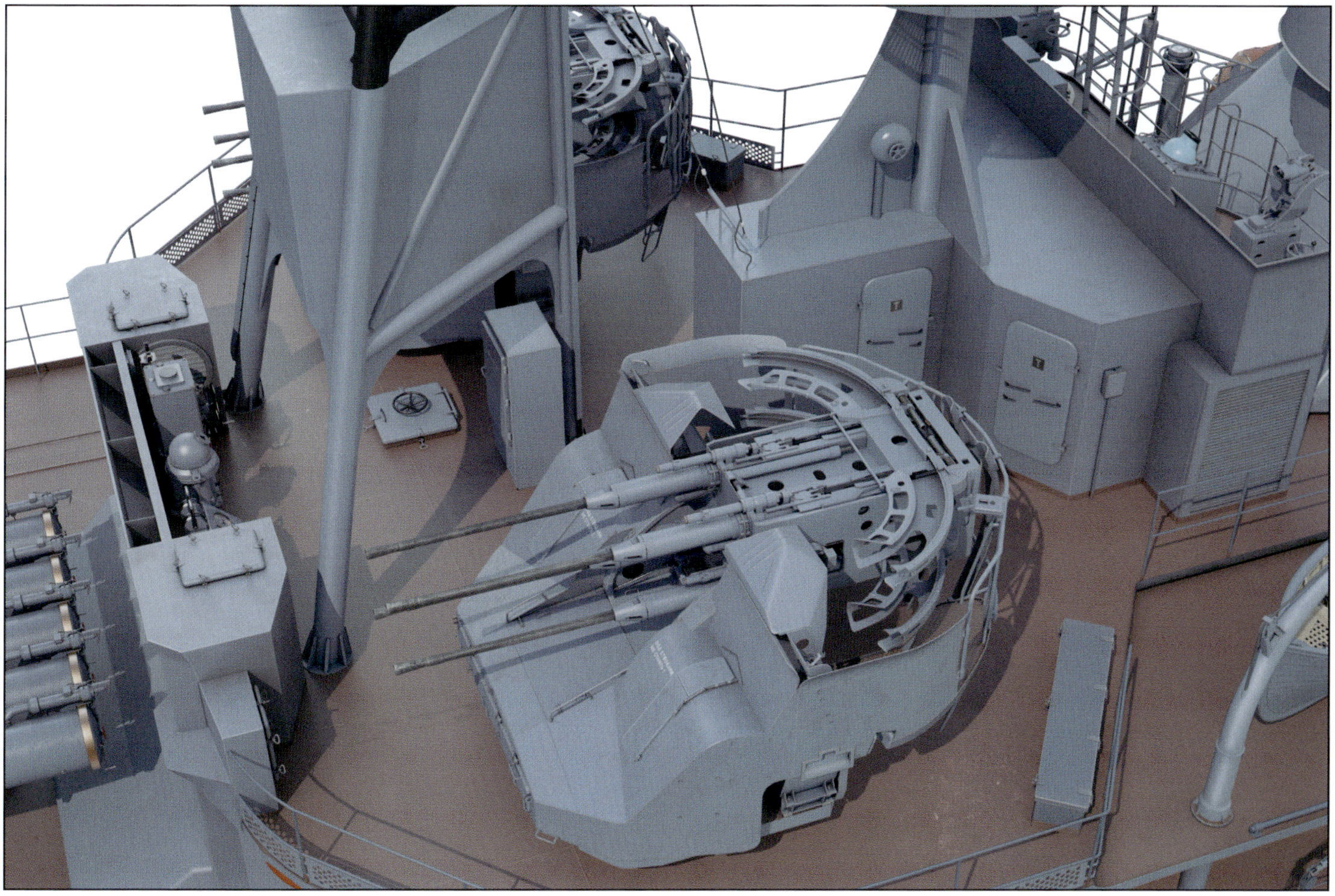

Rear fire control post.

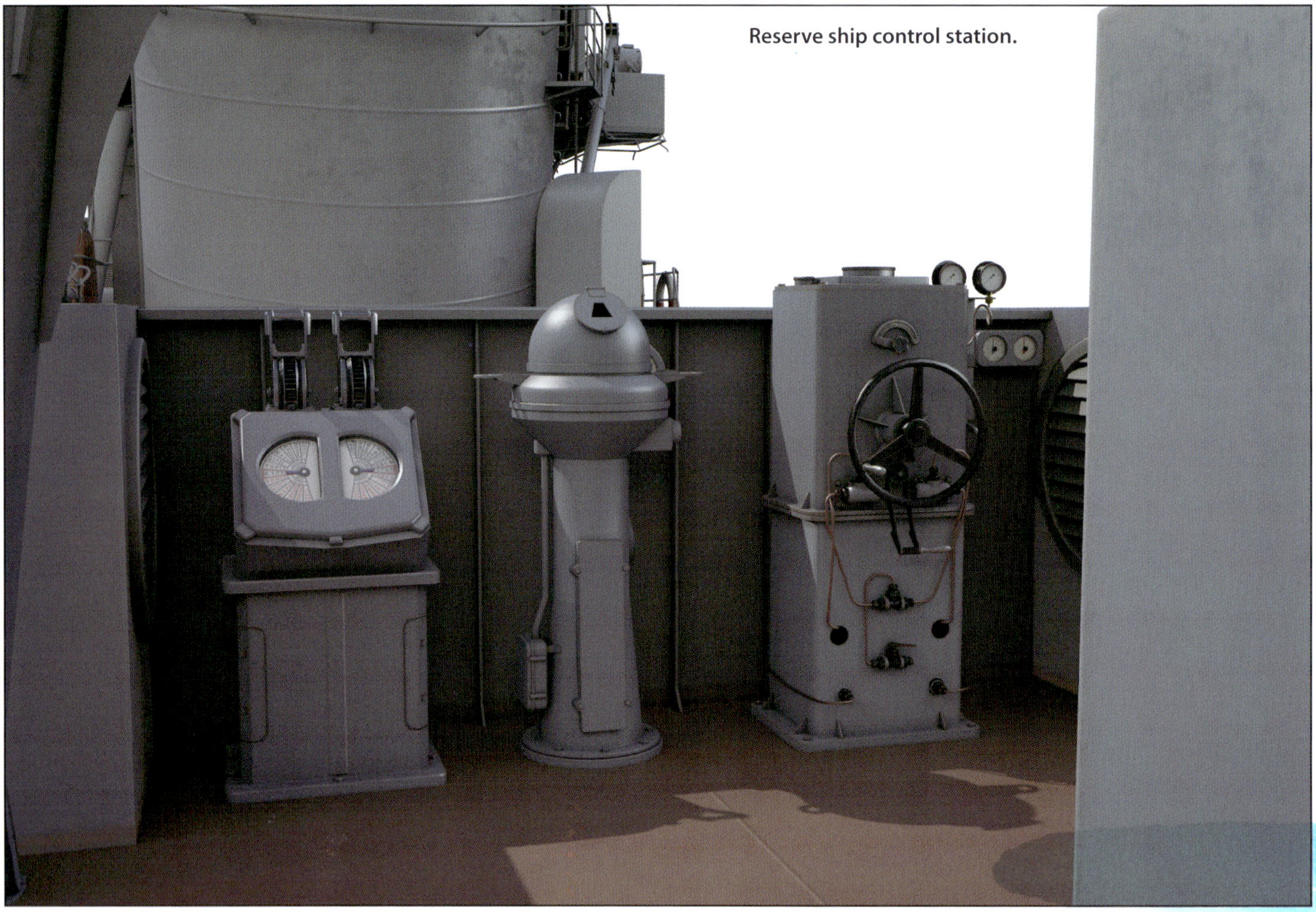

Reserve ship control station.

Reserve ship control station.

The felling of operators "FUT-N" radar.

Friend or Foe System (IFF) antenna.

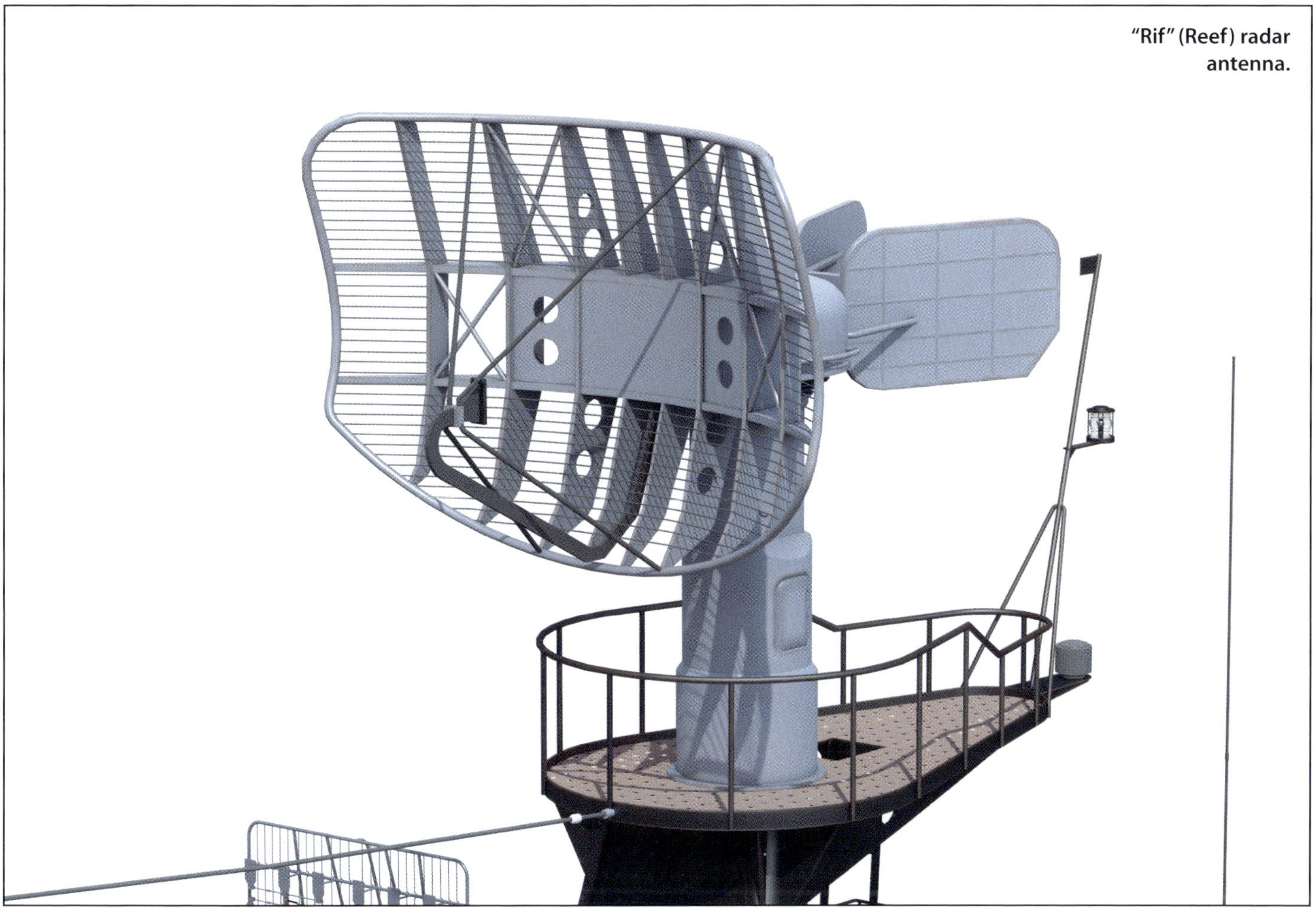

"Rif" (Reef) radar antenna.

The "Fut B" radar of rear hemisphere.

The rear stand fire control post.

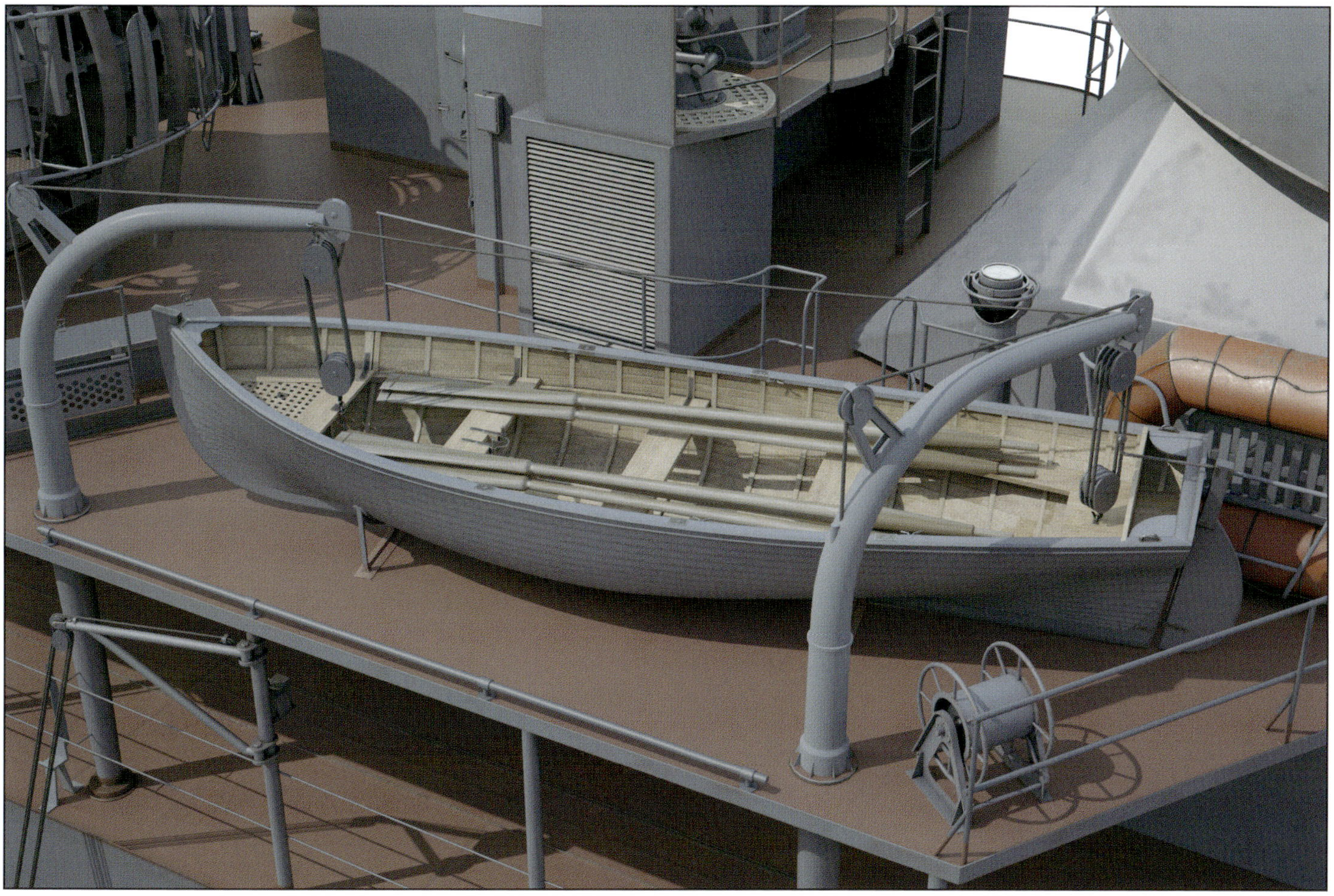

Six-oared yal and davits, port side.

Aft funnel.

Rear part of the midships superstructure. Starboard stern view.

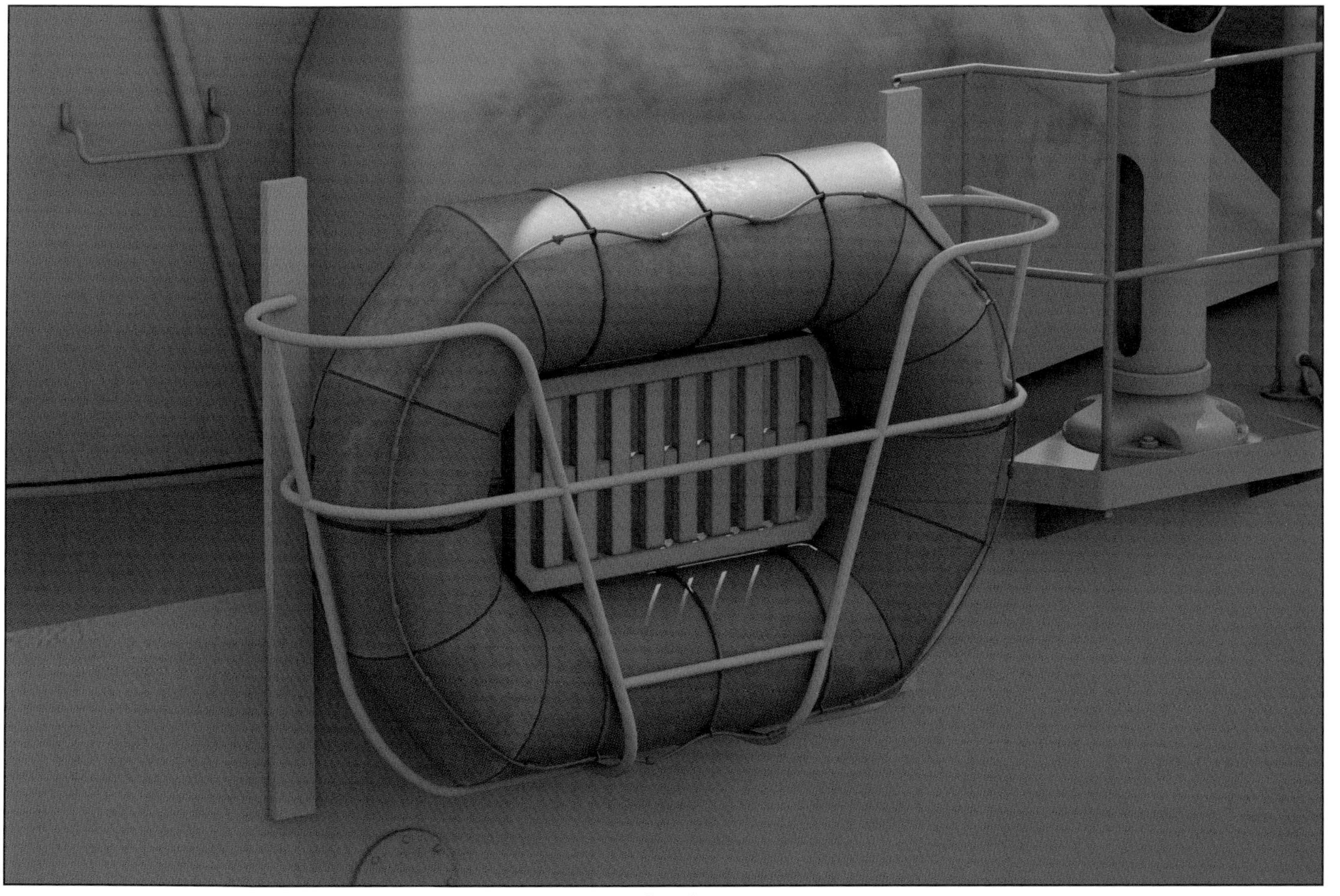

Life raft.

Folded starboard ladder.

Port side ladder.

Rear torpedo launcher.

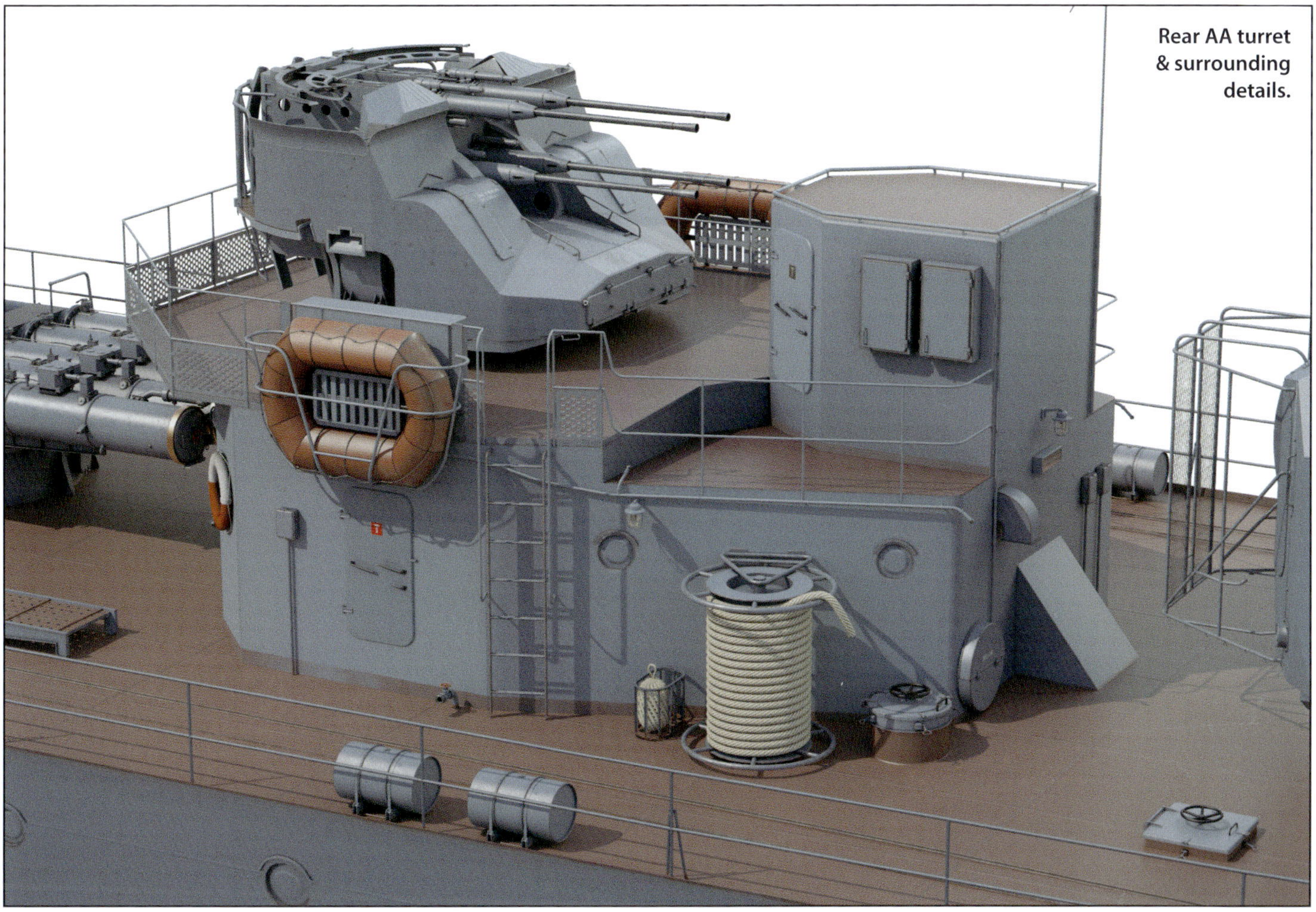

Rear AA turret & surrounding details.

ПРИ

Main rear turret 130 mm & rear stairwell.

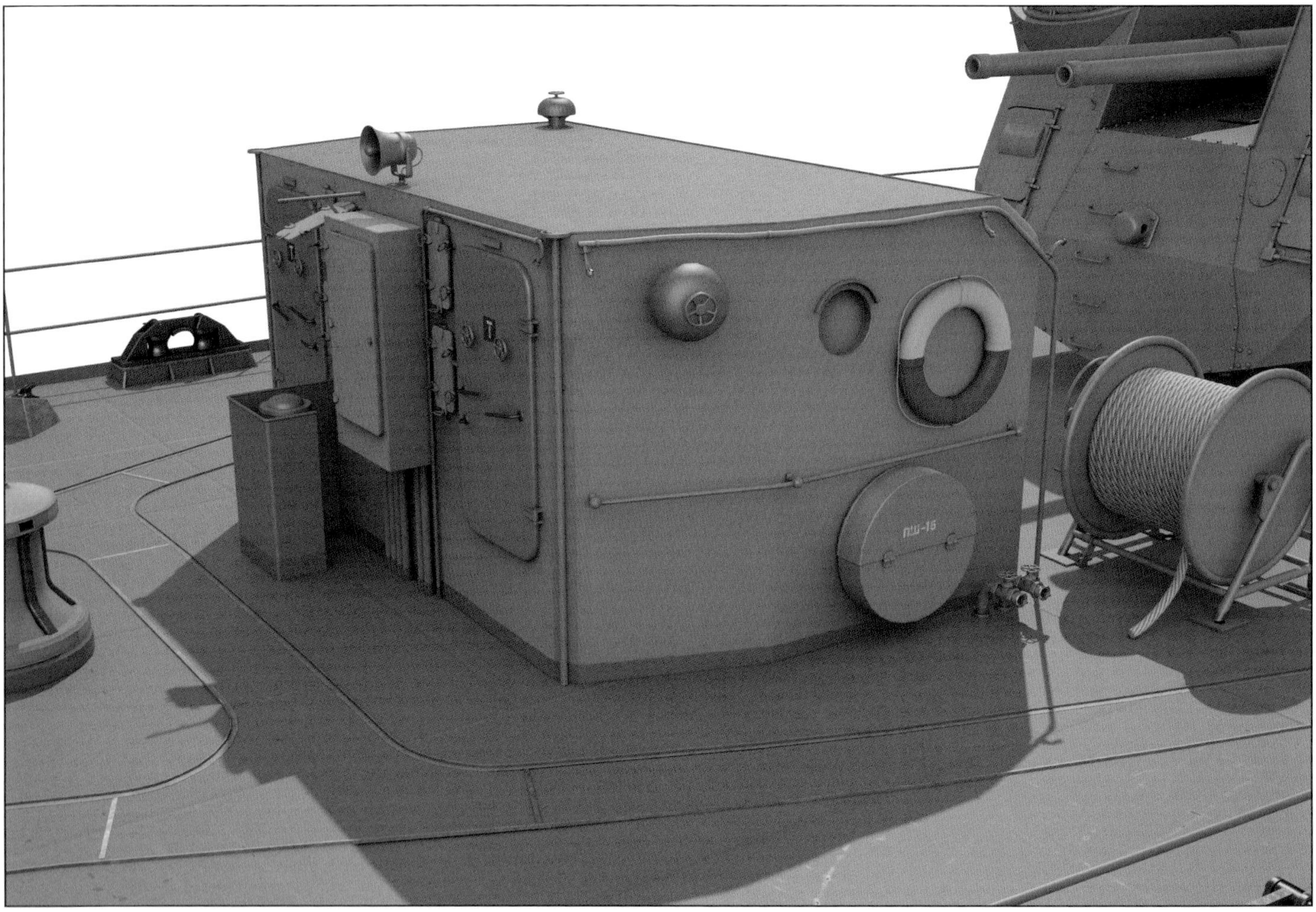

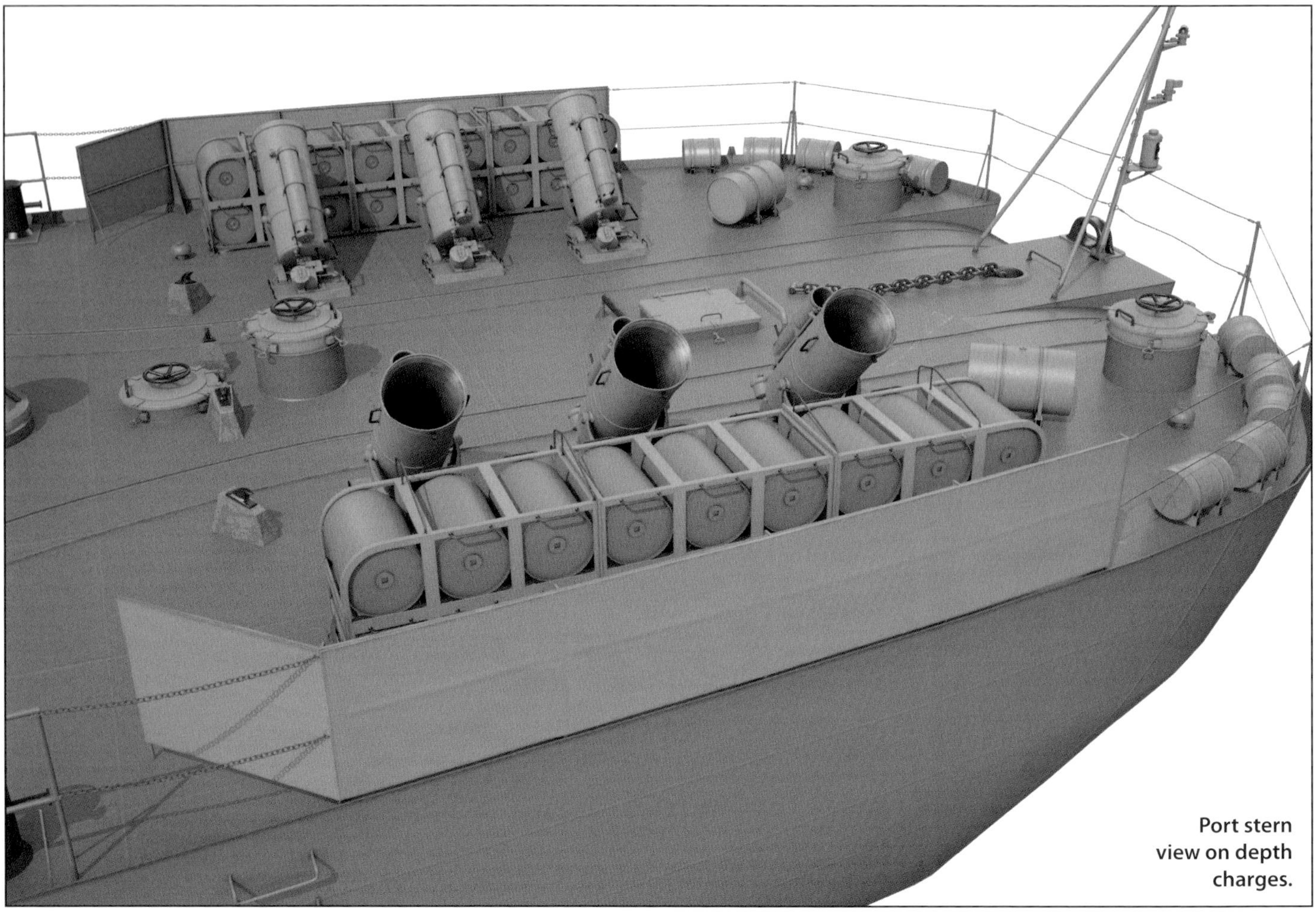

Port stern view on depth charges.

BDSh smoke devices.

Rear flagpole, port stern view.

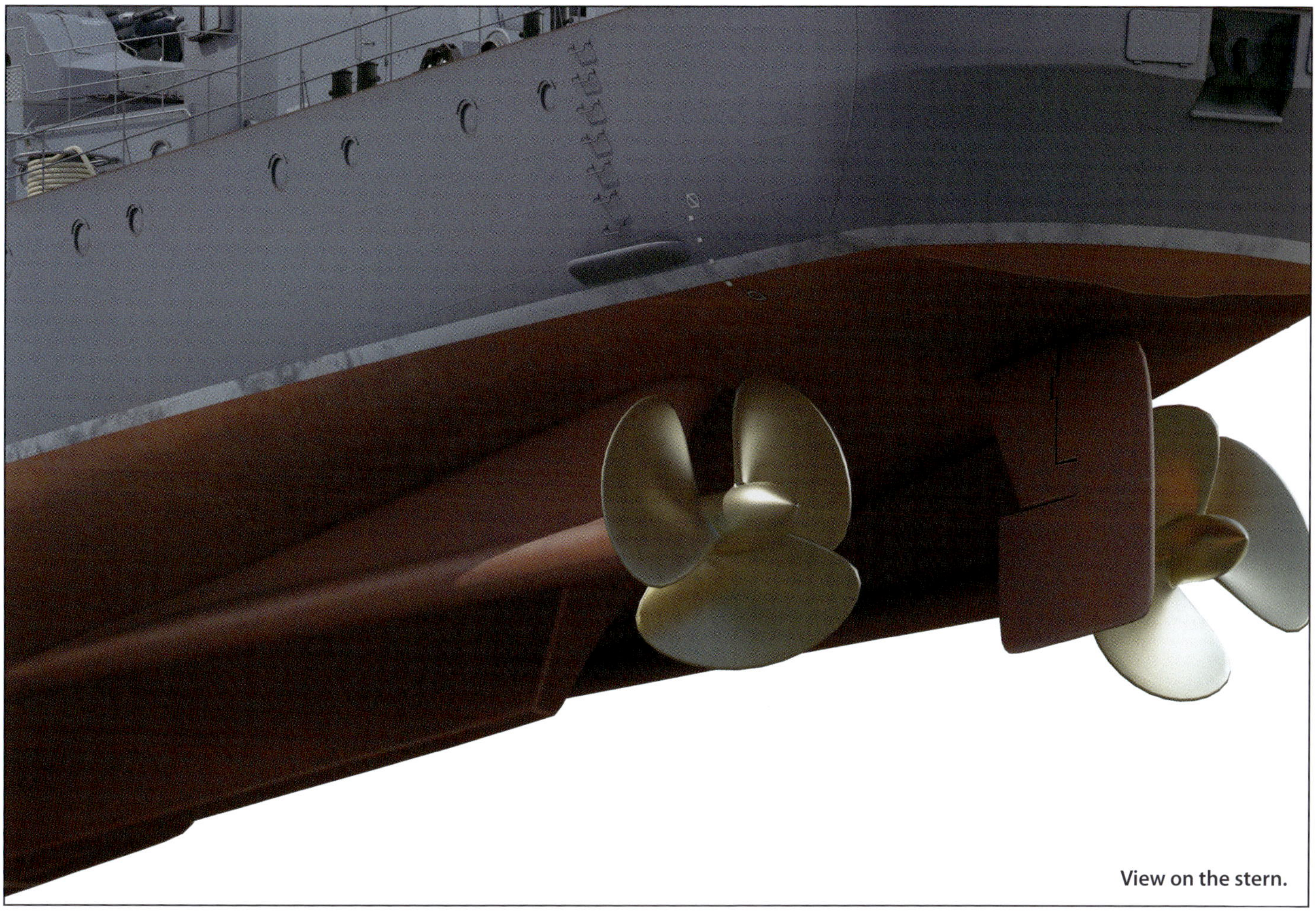
View on the stern.

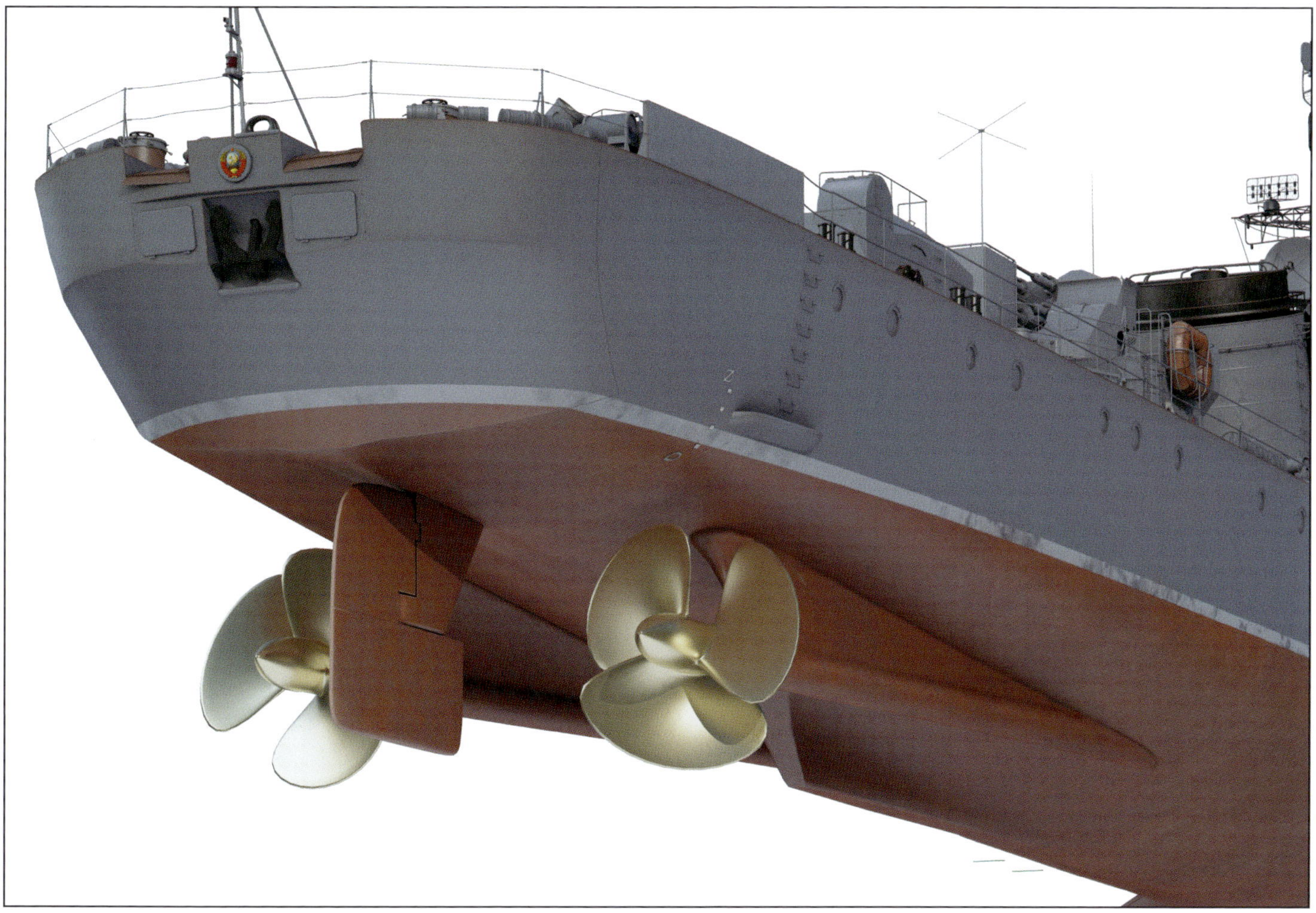

BMB-2 depth charge thrower
and BB-1 depth charge.

The same depth charge
thrower from another side.

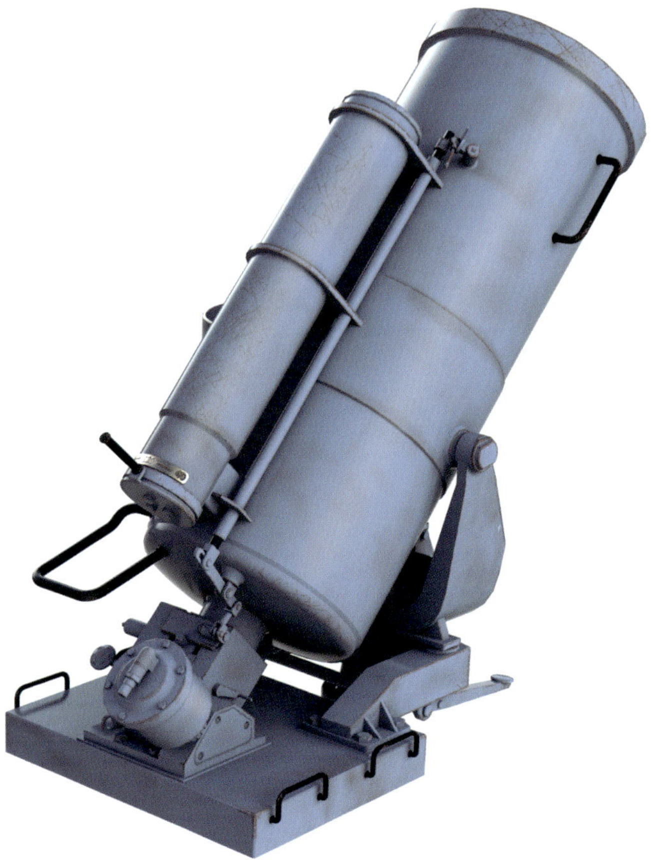

BMB-2 depth charge thrower on mount allowing change of angle of elevation.

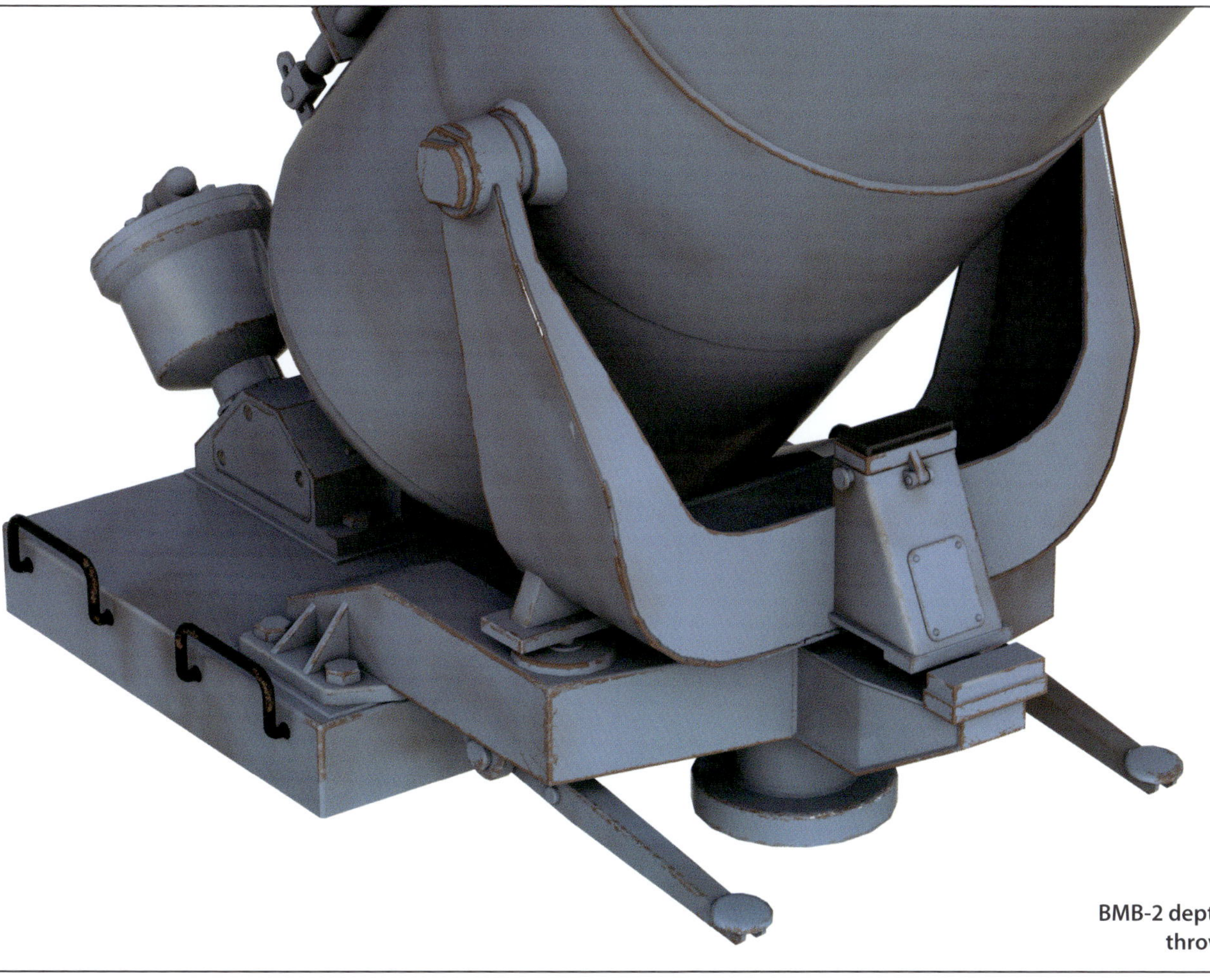

BMB-2 depth charge thrower base.

BMB-2 depth charge thrower base with instrumentation.

BMB-2 depth charge thrower with depth charge container.

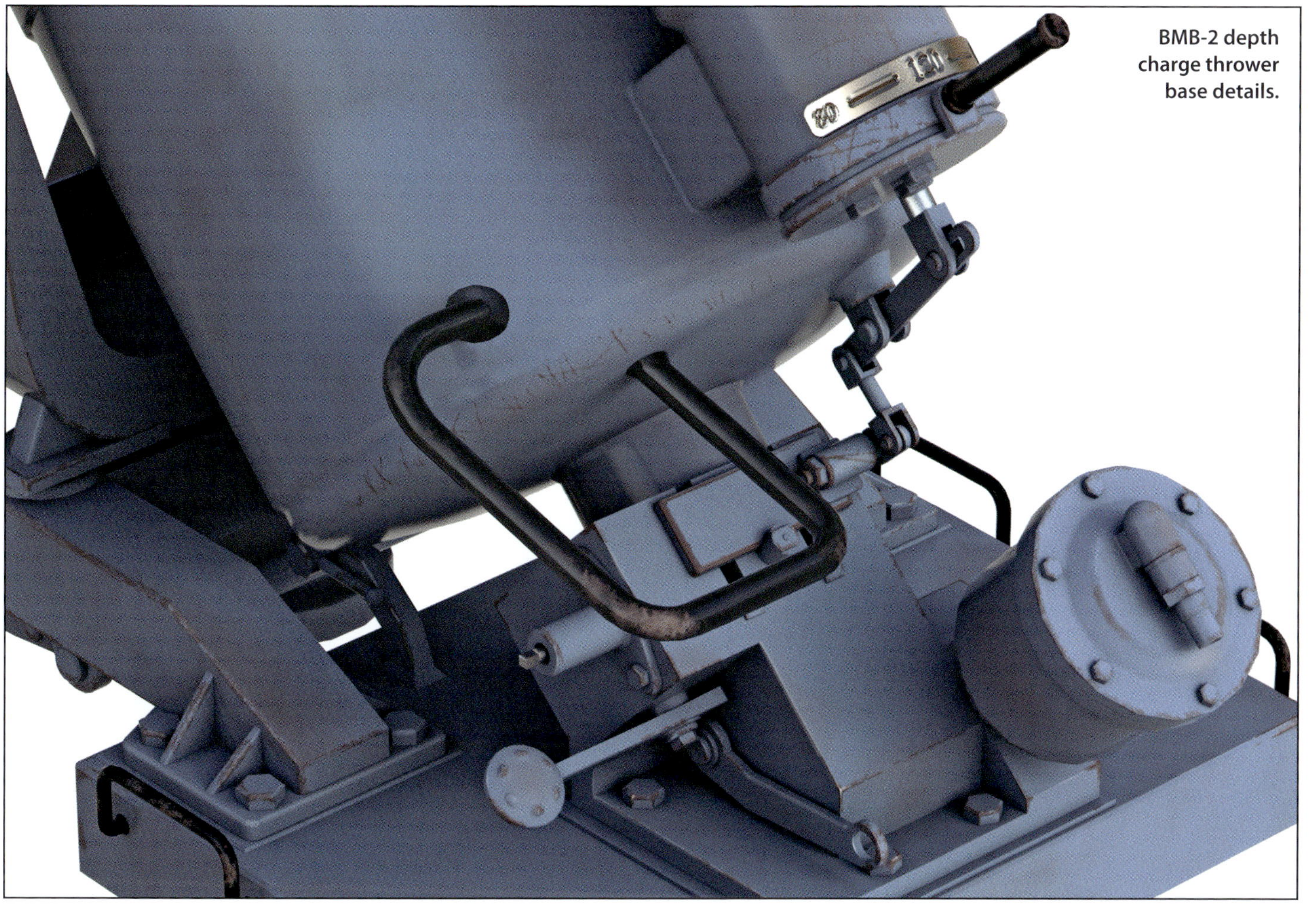

BMB-2 depth charge thrower base details.

BB-1 depth charge with K-3 fuse.

Twin SM-2-1 130 mm gun mount.

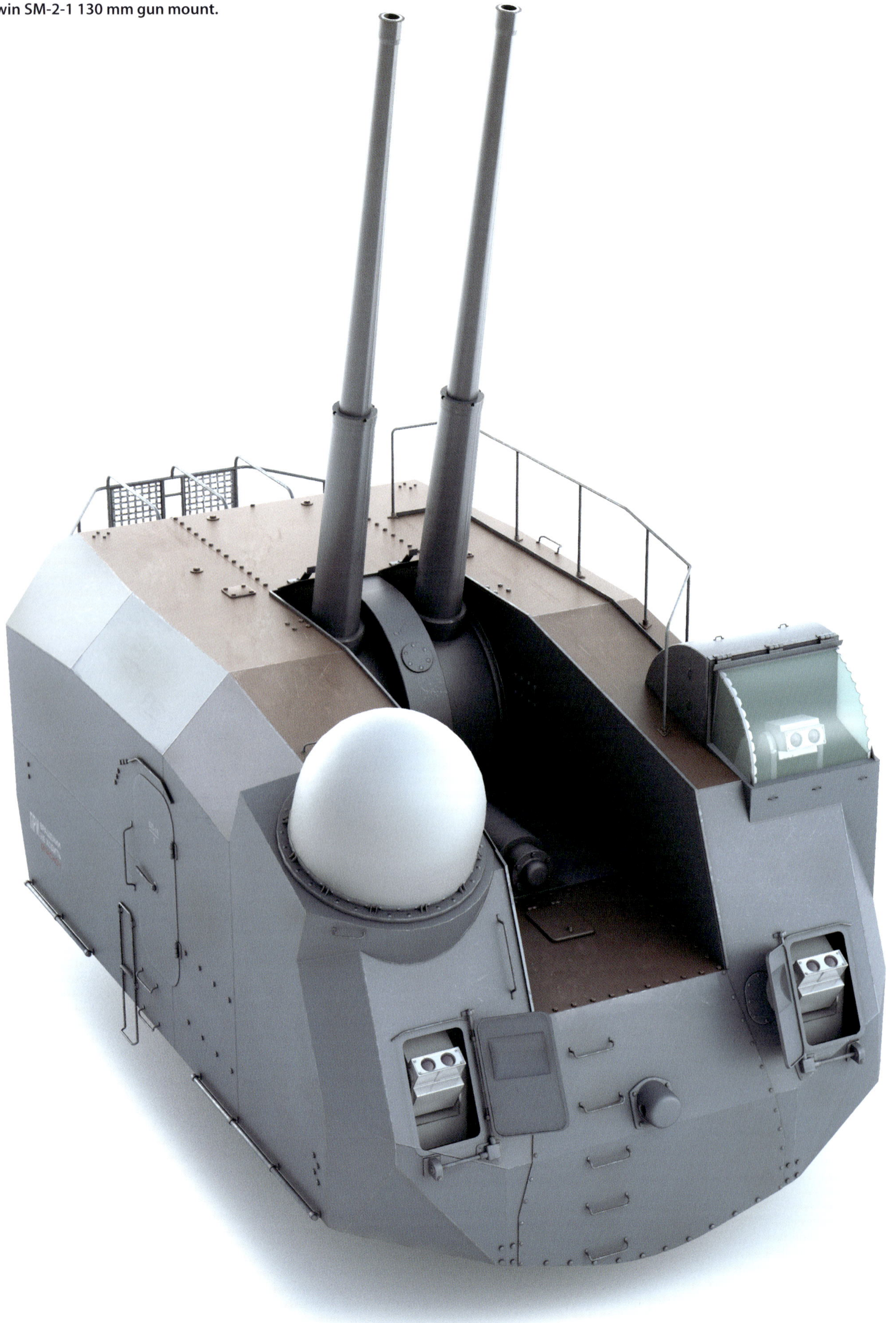

Left side of the SM-2-1 gun mount.

Half-open rear of the SM-2-1 gun mount.

Left side of the SM-2-1 gun mount.

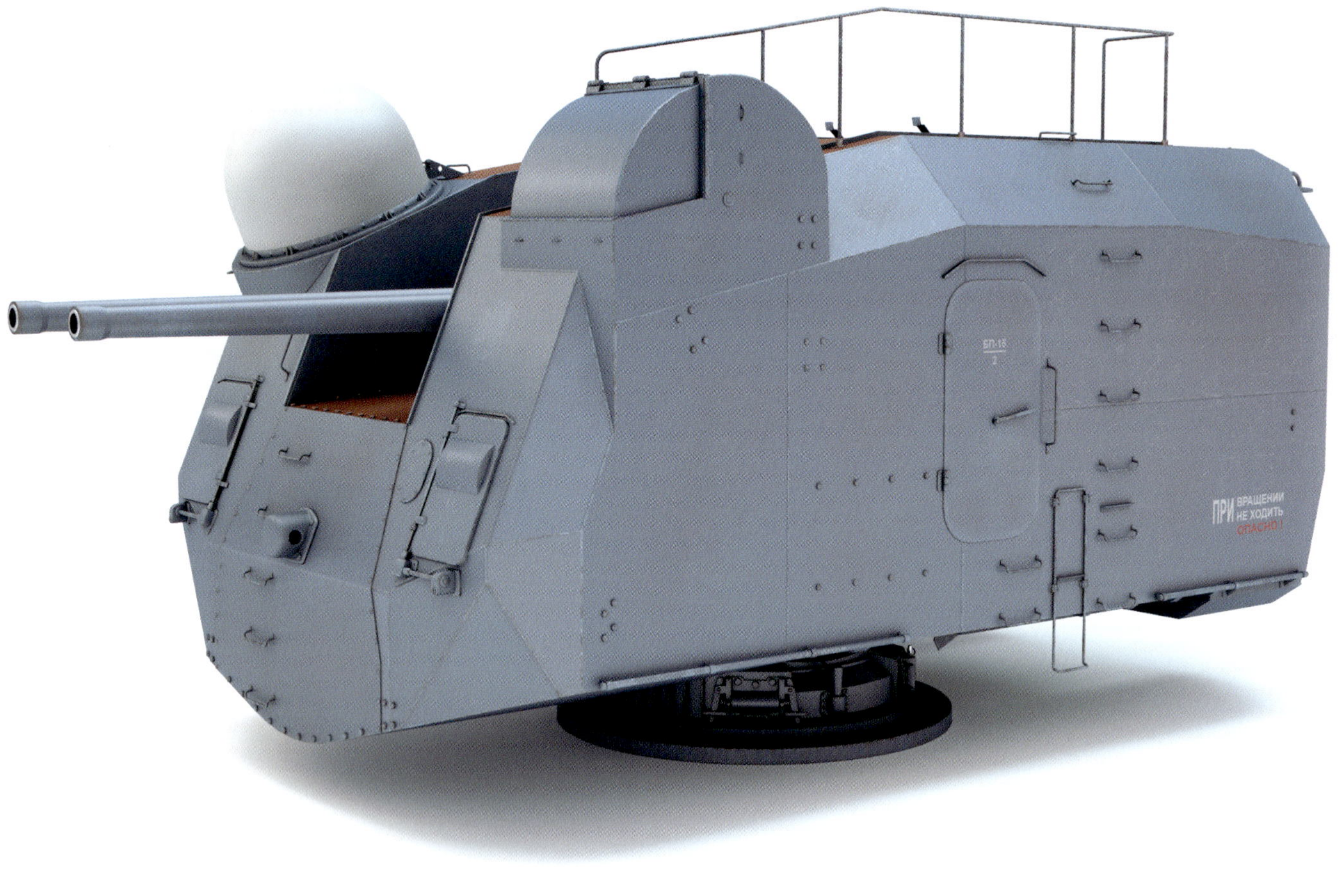

SM-2-1 gun mount with barrels in position "0" with covered ocular observation instruments.

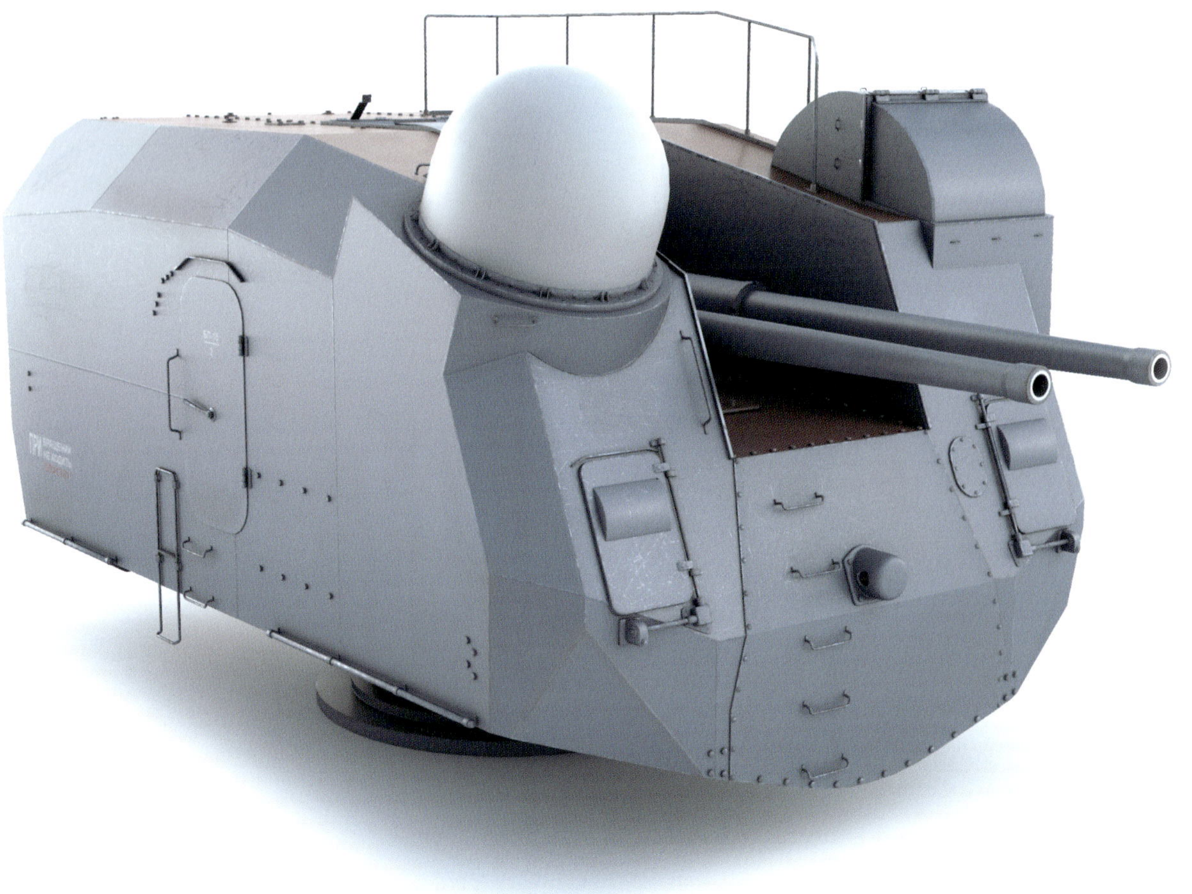

View from the side of quad SM-20-ZIF 45 mm gun mount post.

SM-20-ZIF gun mount post with visible ammunition supply system.

Rare arrangement of quad SM-20-ZIF gun mount.

PTA-53-56 torpedo launcher battery.

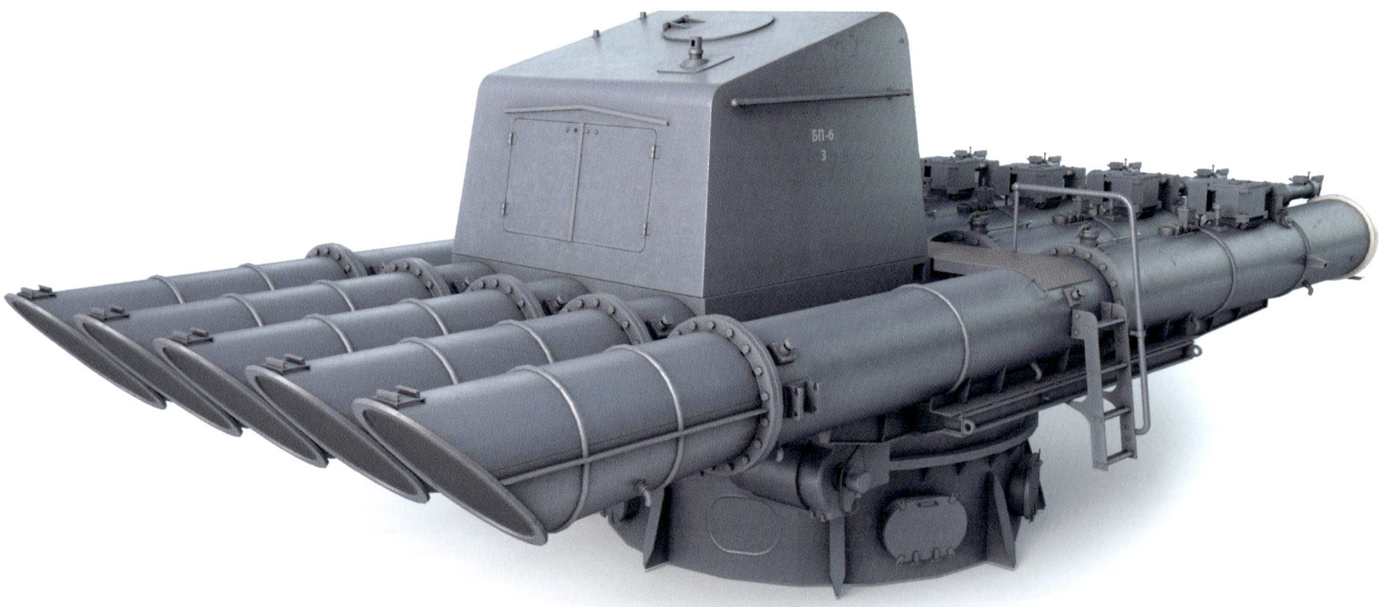

The same torpedo launcher battery seen from the torpedo loading side.

Covered operating station of PTA-53-56 torpedo launchers.

Covers of launchers 4 and 5 with bolting apparatus.

Structural detail of one of the torpedo launchers.

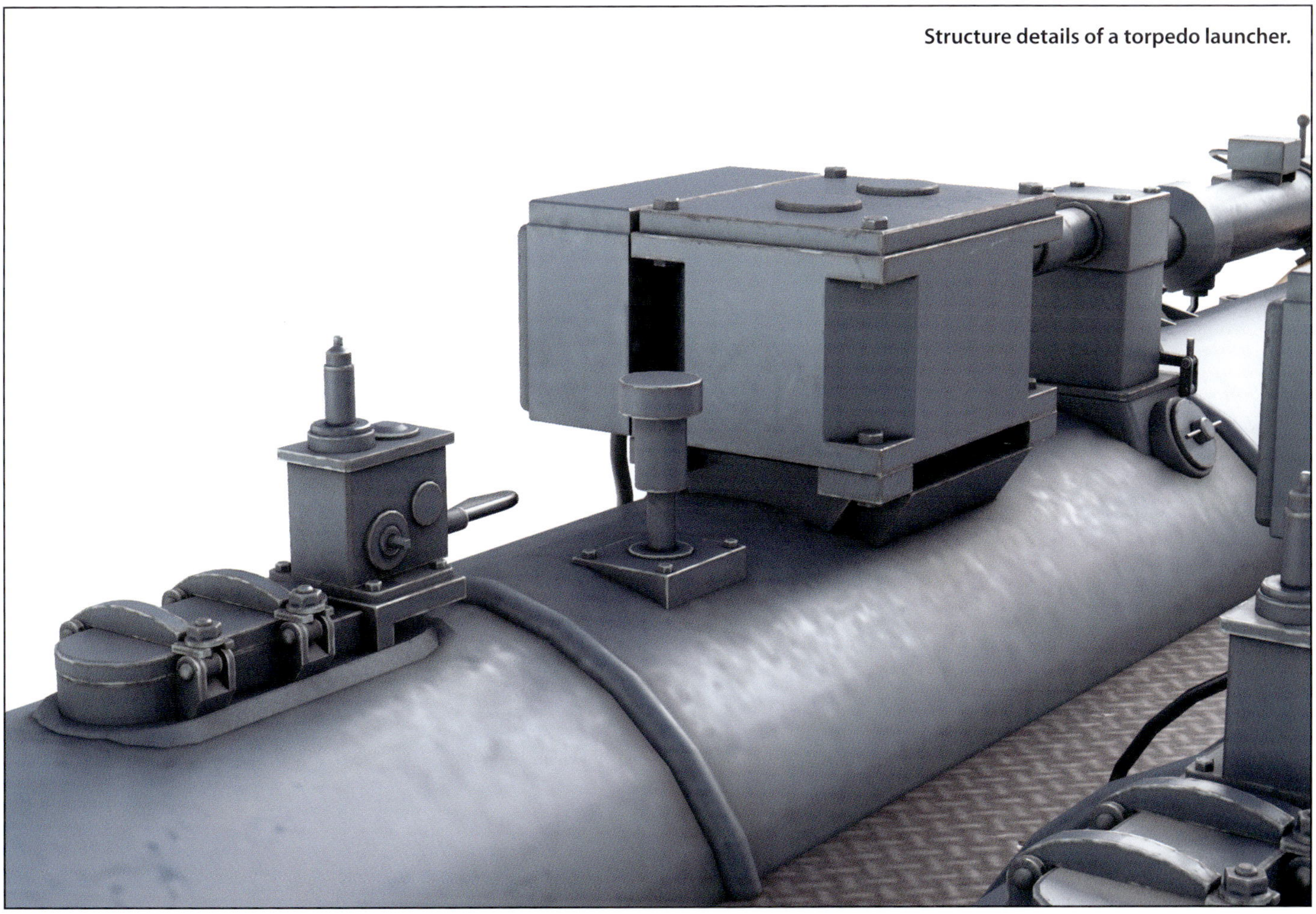
Structure details of a torpedo launcher.

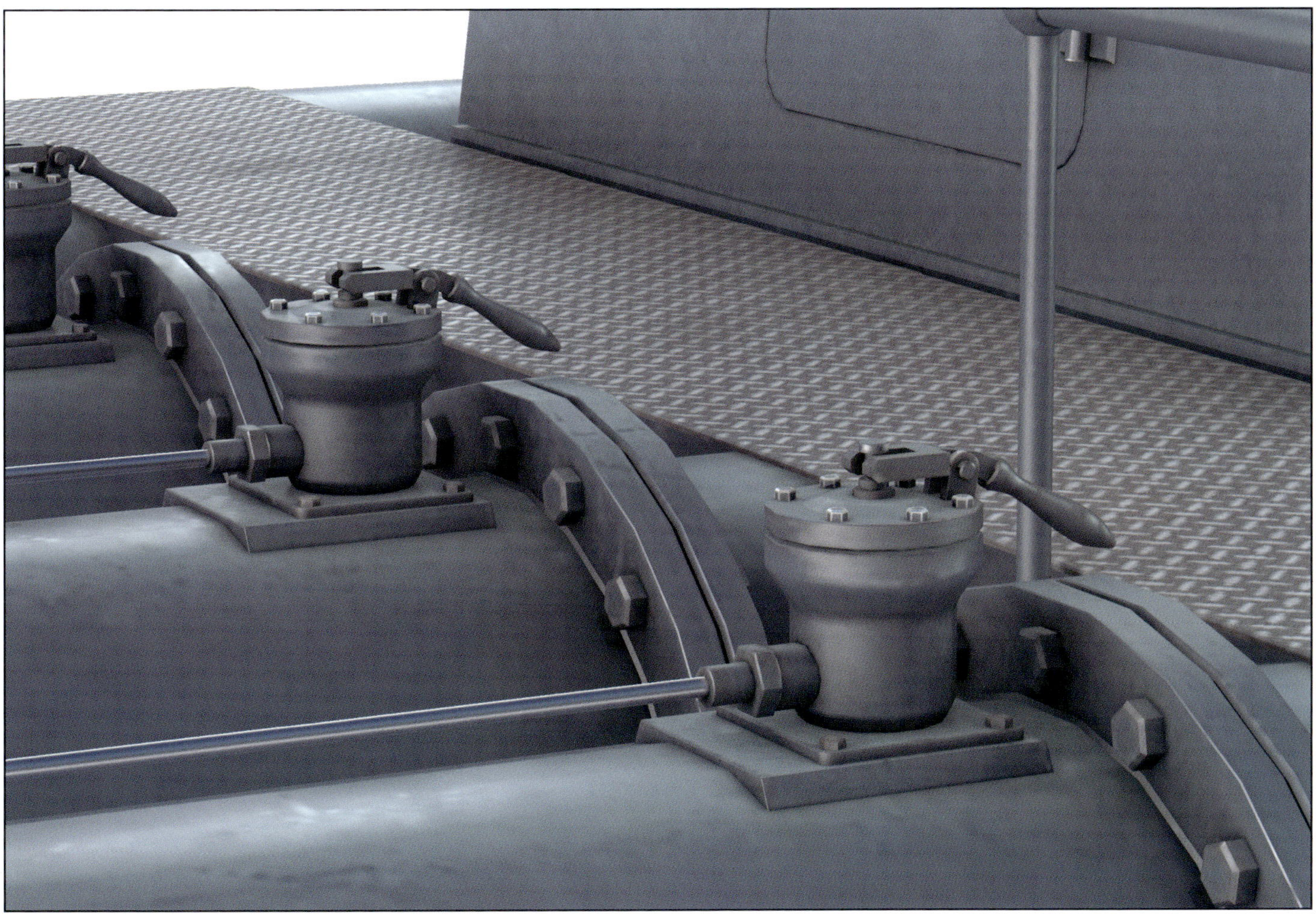

Rotary base of PTA-53-56 launcher.

Destroyer Commander's motor boat proj. 378.

View on the port side of the Commander's boat.

The same boat from the bow side.

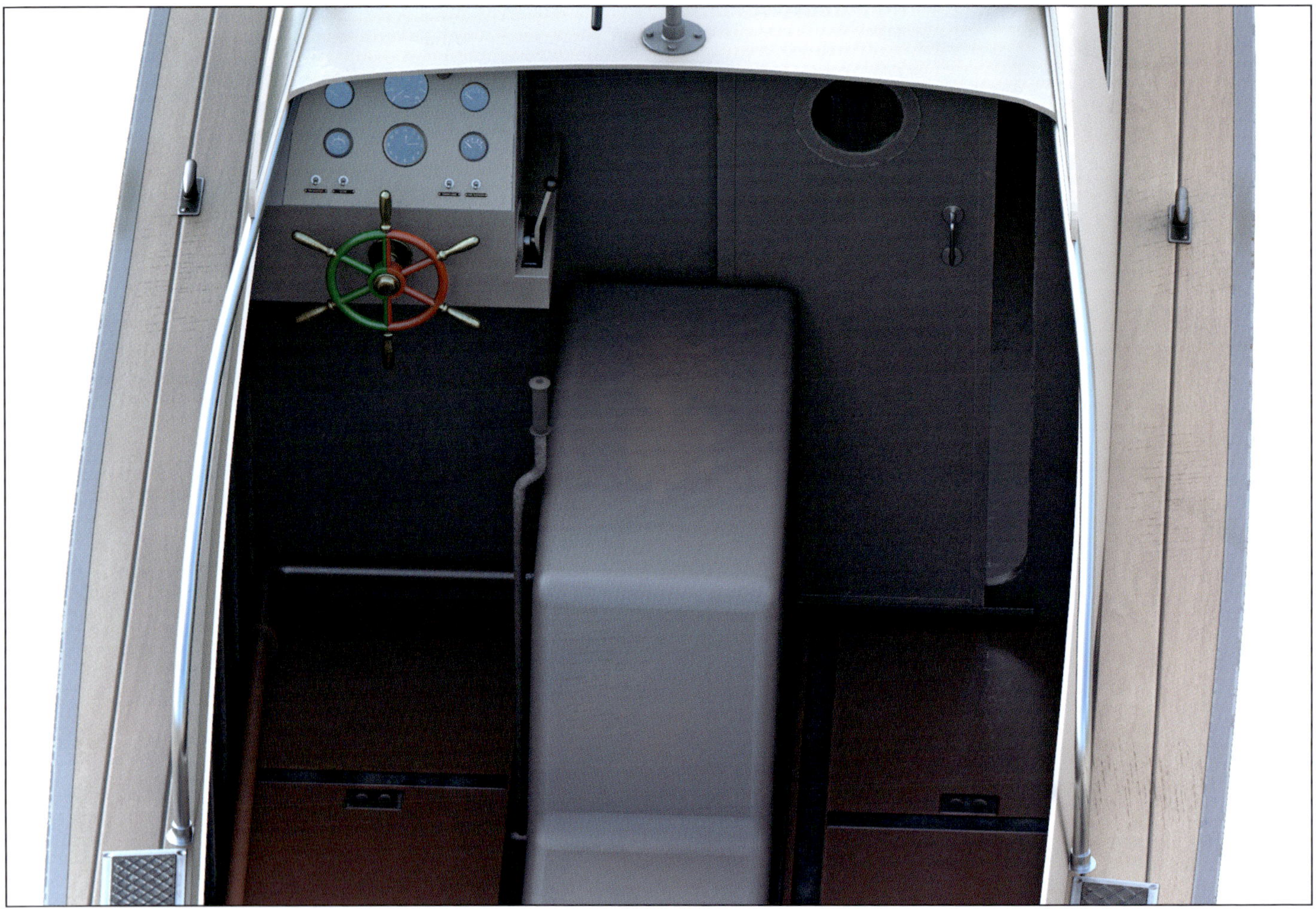

▲
Helmsman's post of the Commander's motor boat.

Work boat (motor launch).

Arial view from the starboard of the work boat.

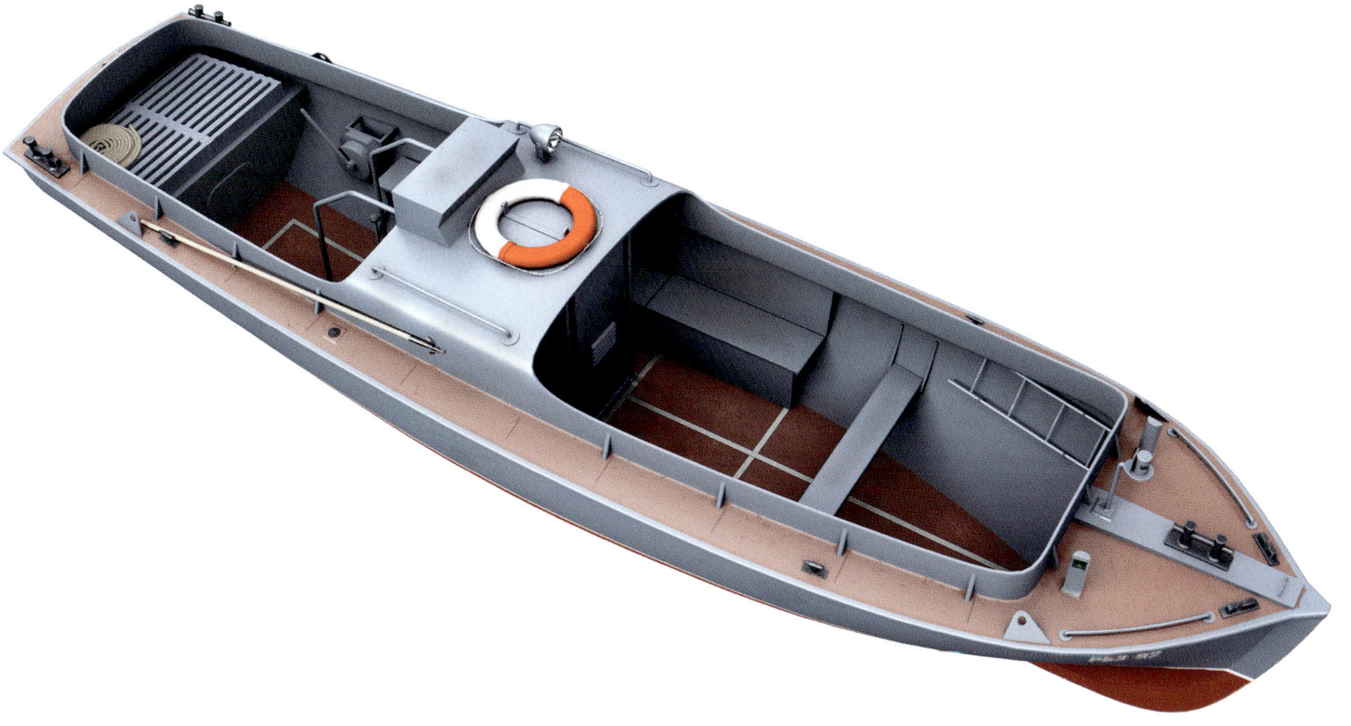

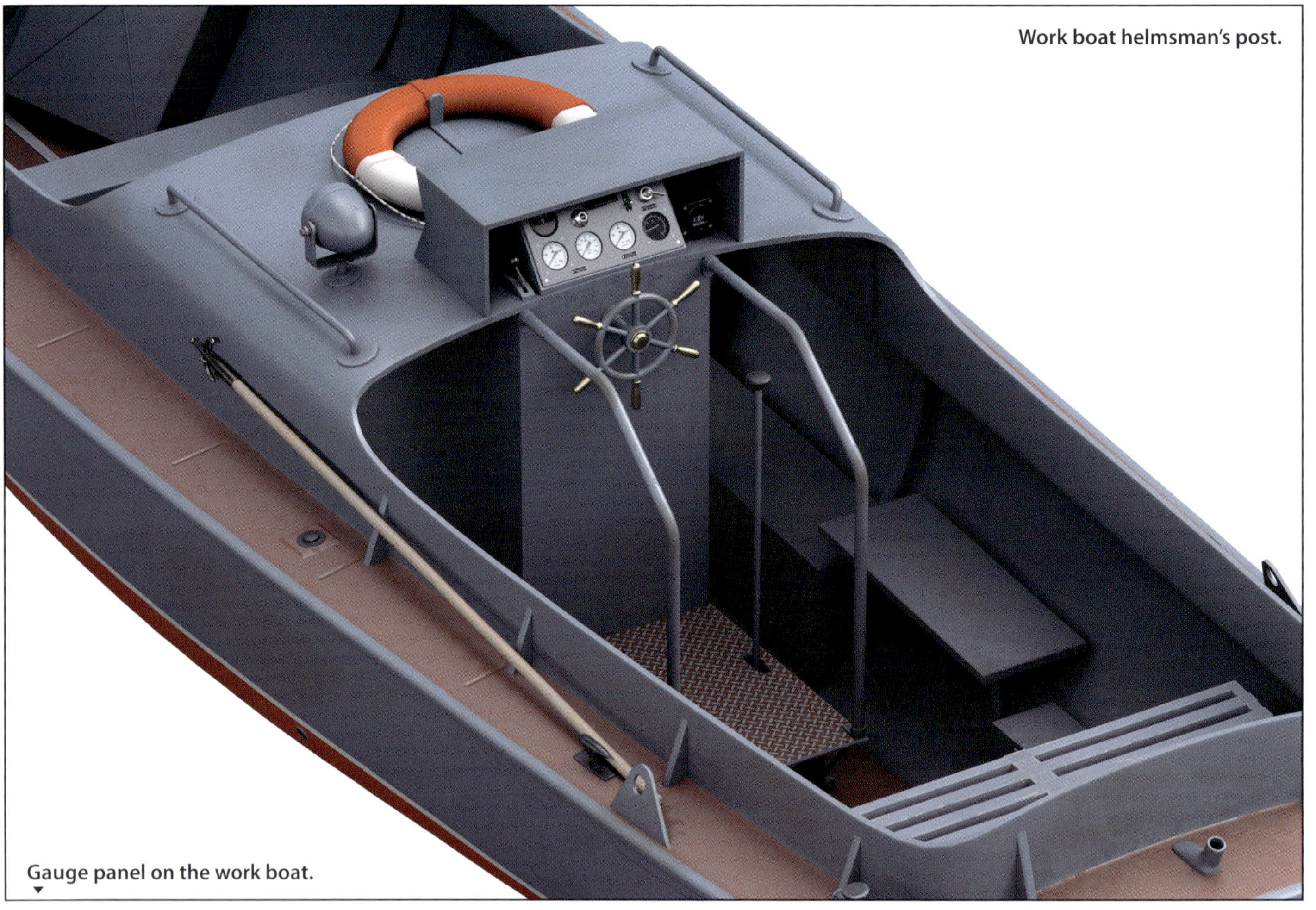
Work boat helmsman's post.

Gauge panel on the work boat.

Bow of the work boat.

Stern of the work boat with the propeller and the wheel.

Six-oared yal type 6.

The same yal seen from thebow side.

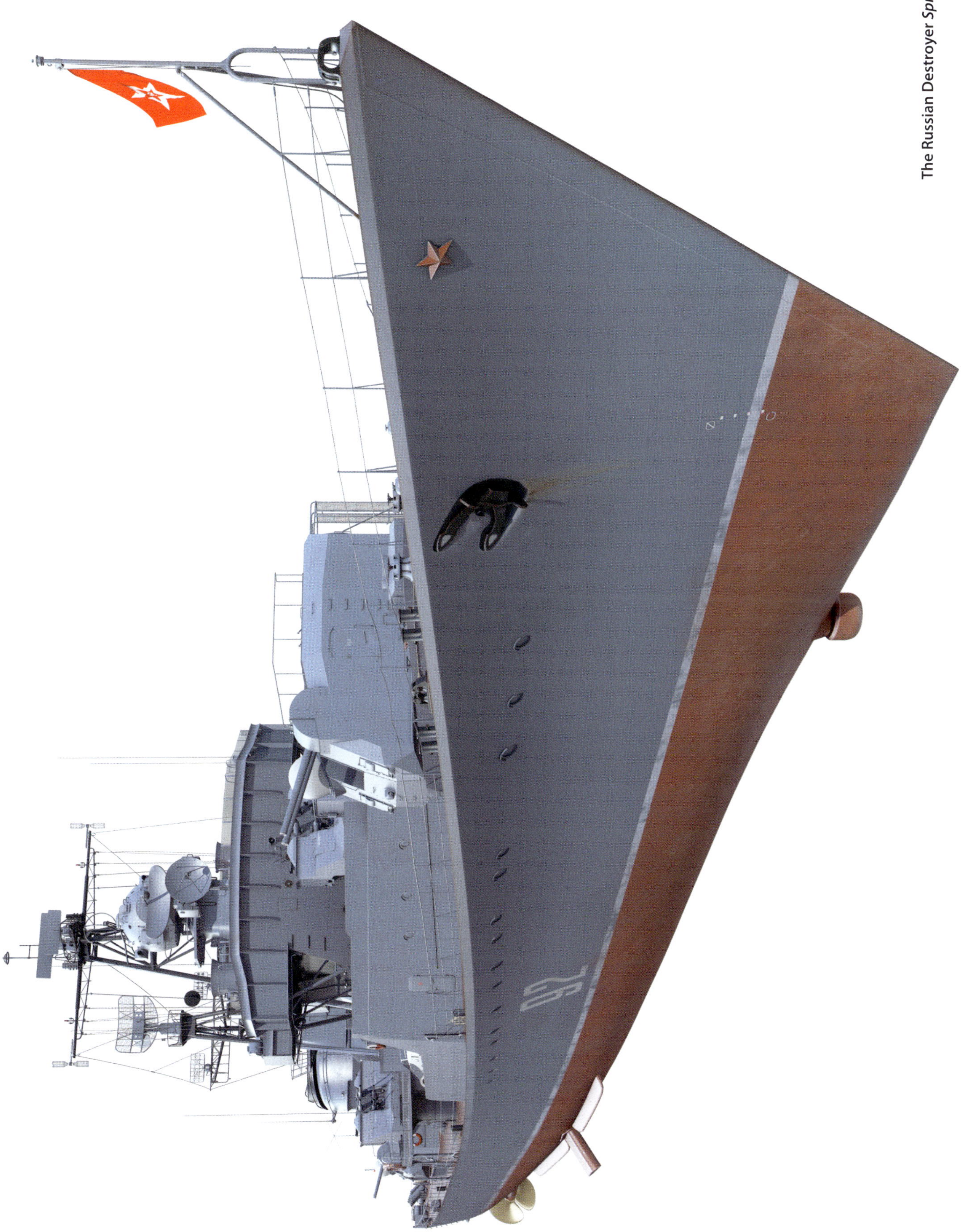

The Russian Destroyer *Spravedlivyy*.
Bow view.

The Russian Destroyer Spravedlivyy 1956 – Oleg Pomoshnikov, Jan Radziemski

LUBLIN 2018 • ISBN 978-83-66148-03-1

3D illustrations: **Oleg Pomoshnikov** • Captions and text: **Jan Radziemski** • Translation: **Łukasz Golowanow (text), Sławomir Judek (captions)** • Design: **KAGERO STUDIO** – Łukasz Maj

KAGERO Publishing • www.kagero.pl, e-mail: kagero@kagero.pl, marketing@kagero.pl

Editorial office, Marketing, Distribution: KAGERO Publishing, Akacjowa 100, os. Borek, Turka, 20-258 Lublin 62, Poland, phone/fax (+48) 81 501 21 05

w w w . k a g e r o . e u

3D visualisations are based on the available photographs, drawings and other archive data, and should be treated only as author's attempt to recreate the original look of the particular machine as faithfully as possible. If you are in possession of materials to which author did not reach, and you would like to help us to develop a better publication, please contact the Publisher on: redakcja@kagero.pl